At Issue

| Space Exploration

Other Books in the At Issue Series:

At Issue

Space Exploration

David Haugen and Zack Lewis, Book Editors

GREENHAVEN PRESS
A part of Gale, Cengage Learning

GALE
CENGAGE Learning™

Detroit • New York • San Francisco • New Haven, Conn • Waterville, Maine • London

GALE
CENGAGE Learning™

Elizabeth Des Chenes, *Managing Editor*

© 2012 Greenhaven Press, a part of Gale, Cengage Learning

Gale and Greenhaven Press are registered trademarks used herein under license.

For more information, contact:
Greenhaven Press
27500 Drake Rd.
Farmington Hills, MI 48331-3535
Or you can visit our Internet site at gale.cengage.com

For product information and technology assistance, contact us at

Gale Customer Support, 1-800-877-4253
For permission to use material from this text or product, submit all requests online at www.cengage.com/permissions

Further permissions questions can be emailed to permissionrequest@cengage.com

Articles in Greenhaven Press anthologies are often edited for length to meet page requirements. In addition, original titles of these works are changed to clearly present the main thesis and to explicitly indicate the author's opinion. Every effort is made to ensure that Greenhaven Press accurately reflects the original intent of the authors. Every effort has been made to trace the owners of copyrighted material.

Cover image © Images.com/Corbis.

LIBRARY OF CONGRESS CATALOGING-IN-PUBLICATION DATA

Space exploration / David Haugen and Zack Lewis, book editors.
    p. cm. -- (At issue)
    Includes bibliographical references and index.
    ISBN 978-0-7377-5596-1 (hardback) -- ISBN 978-0-7377-5597-8 (paperback)
  1. Outer space--Exploration. I. Haugen, David M., 1969- II. Lewis, Zack (Zack T.)
    QB500.262.S622 2011
    629.4--dc23

                                      2011018846

Printed in the United States of America
1 2 3 4 5 6 7 15 14 13 12 11

Contents

Introduction

On the heels of World War II (1939-1945), former allies, the Soviet Union and the United States, engaged in a new power struggle known as the Cold War, marked by political maneuvering, arms development, athletic competition, and most famously the so-called Space Race. Researching a means to use rockets to propel objects into space, Americans believed themselves to be at the forefront of world technology and thus leaders in the Space Race. They were caught off guard, however, in 1957 by the Soviet launch of Sputnik, the first man-made satellite to be put into orbit. Frantically, the United States redoubled its efforts to overcome its communist rivals and reclaim the technological lead. The Soviets were unwilling to concede the advantage, and what followed was an era defined by rapid scientific progress and discovery as the two world powers competed for the conquest of space.

Throughout the Space Race, scientific milestones were achieved and surpassed in quick succession. Shortly after Sputnik, the United States launched its own satellite in 1958, only to be trumped four years later as the Soviet Union sent the first manned spacecraft into orbit. Weeks later, the United States would launch its first astronaut but would not succeed in establishing a manned orbital craft for another year. The Soviet victory in manned spaceflight prompted then-President John F. Kennedy to set an ultimatum for the successful landing of an American on the surface of the moon by the start of 1970. He told an assembly at Rice University in 1962, "We choose to go to the moon in this decade and do the other things, not because they are easy, but because they are hard, because that goal will serve to organize and measure the best of our energies and skills, because that challenge is one that we are willing to accept, one we are unwilling to postpone, and one which we intend to win, and the others, too." Though he did not live to see it, his promise was fulfilled on July 20, 1969, with the successful lunar landing of Apollo 11 and its three-man crew of Neil Armstrong, Buzz Aldrin, and Michael Collins. The feat seemed to reestablish America's lead in the Space Race, though both the United States and the Soviet Union would continue to expand upon past achievements in the decades to come.

Since the moon landing, there have been more than 270 successful manned space missions launched by the United States alone, and in 1975 the Soviet Union and the United States cooperated in the first joint space flight, signaling a turning point in Cold War rivalry. Then, in 1998, the United States, in cooperation with Russia and China, began construction of an International Space Station (ISS). The ISS serves as an orbital laboratory where nations cooperate in performing various experiments in microgravity. First visited by an international crew of astronauts in 2000 and still in service and under construction as of 2011, the ISS is the site of the longest uninterrupted period of human presence in space and the most expensive space project to date. The ISS clearly presented the world with a new vision. No longer was space a battleground of Cold War policies but a shared horizon to be explored by people of many nations.

In an August 2010 issue of *Space Policy*, Sanjoy Som, a member of the Department of Earth and Space Sciences at the University of Washington, stated, "The International Space Station (ISS) is a great example of what can be accomplished through sustained international collaboration." He expects that such joint missions will continue to earn the goodwill and backing of all people so that humanity's interest in the new frontier will not flag. As Som maintains, "The success of a long-term space program is linked, directly and indirectly, to the excitement, enthusiasm and awareness of the supporting general public." In the United States, interest in the space program and space technology has remained high, yet Americans are aware of the costs the country has borne. The US space program suffered major setbacks in both 1986 and 2003 with the loss of space shuttles *Challenger* and *Columbia* and their respective crews. The failure of a hydrogen fuel tank caused the *Challenger* to disintegrate seventy-three seconds into the launch of its tenth mission, resulting in a two-year hiatus and investigation of the National Aeronautics and Space Administration (NASA). In 2003, damage to the *Columbia*'s heat shield during launch led to the shuttle's destruction as it re-entered Earth's atmosphere. These tragedies cast severe doubt among the public about whether such ventures into space were worth the cost of human life and the tax dollars used to fund NASA missions. Some observers speculate that these disasters may have influenced President Barack Obama's 2010 decision to cancel NASA's Constellation program, which aimed to return astronauts to the moon.

Despite such setbacks, a majority of Americans still find value in the space program. A July 2009 Gallup poll found that 63 percent of adults between 18 and 49 years of age and 54 percent of those over 50 believe the space program has brought enough benefits to the country to justify its costs. At the same time, the polling agency reported that Americans' support for increasing or maintaining NASA's budget has steadily declined since 2003. Experts explain that the decline is likely due to the 2008 recession and an increasing focus on the financial burdens of health care and the national deficit. Because of rising unemployment and the difficulty of making ends meet, Americans are less enthusiastic about pouring billions of dollars into a program that may not have immediate results, at least in their daily lives. Some believe NASA must adapt to this reality. As journalist Jonathan Penn writes in the December 6, 2010, issue of *Aviation Week & Space Technology*, "Without radical rethinking and restructuring, the space program will not garner the public support it needs to survive the current economic doldrums and will be unable to help the

US remain a technology leader in the 21st century." Others have argued for the complete elimination of the space program, concentrating government science instead on the as-yet unexplored regions of Earth or shifting tax dollars to social welfare programs for those in need.

In *At Issue: Space Exploration*, scientists, politicians, science fiction writers, and even the early spacefarers themselves voice their thoughts on what space exploration holds in store for Earth's inhabitants in viewpoints that debate the utility of NASA, the benefits of international cooperation, and the anticipated need to colonize other planets. There are no easy answers to these debates that question whether the future of humanity lies in the stars or here on Earth.

1

Space Exploration Is Inspirational and Educational

Buzz Aldrin, interviewed by Vikas Shah

A former US Air Force pilot, Buzz Aldrin became an astronaut for the burgeoning National Aeronautics and Space Administration (NASA) in 1963. He helped devise important spacecraft docking equipment and became famous in 1966 for making the first spacewalk from the Gemini 12 orbital mission. He subsequently joined the 1969 Apollo 11 mission and gained further notoriety as the second astronaut to walk on the moon. Since his retirement from the Air Force and NASA in 1972, he has remained an ardent supporter of the US space program. Vikas Shah is an entrepreneur who leads Thought Strategy, a strategy consulting and advisory firm.

Space exploration has definite benefits for humanity. It can provide access to new resources, such as scarce elements and minerals, and it may offer the best hope for the survival of humankind if the earth suffers some cosmic or terrestrial calamity. Analyzing other planets and stellar bodies also may teach humans much about Earth's natural systems; and humanity's ingenuity in overcoming problems posed by space travel might be used to solve potential crises on Earth. Furthermore, space exploration can provide young people with the motivation to learn about the universe and perhaps push them into the sciences and mathematical fields—two educational arenas that countries, including the United States, will need to develop to remain competitive in the future.

[V]ikas Shah]: *What is the economic role and significance of space exploration in our civilisation's future?*

Buzz Aldrin: I think the aerospace industries of the U.S. and all nations will gain from considering the return from, for example, satellite reconnaissance, and many other areas that I'll touch on.

Reconnaissance and defence in particular though, are important not just for offensive operations, but to maintain peace. The more one knows about potential adversaries, their resources, and their abilities to damage the economics of other nations, for example, is the real return from reconnaissance activities. A missile launched upwards as high as possible, instead of "at a target", which then detonates a nuclear device, could cripple most all of the low earth orbit satellites. This would be detrimental to all nations, especially those who rely so heavily on space assets. Defending against these kinds of attacks is hugely dependent on the health of the aerospace industries. As far as the United States is concerned, we have a history of being defensive of liberty and freedom throughout the world, and I want to stress that we have a lot of assets up there so we, in particular, need to stress the importance of these issues, with encouragement and co-operation of international organisations rather than just those who are critical of the weaponisation of space. At the opposite end of the defence spectrum, we have the issues concerning the survival of economies and major assets on the surface of the earth. This may depend on our ability to detect and defend against impacts from outer space which could be very damaging to entire civilisations, and major portions of the earth. In space, to advance to a point where we have planetary defence is a significant and important option for us.

The resources of the earth are not limitless. We are finding, through scouting, resources and minerals that are located on spotty locations around our planet. These did not all come from the core of the earth, but from the impact of objects with the earth. Those objects also impacted the Moon, and many of them have not yet done so. These objects are, of course, asteroids. The easiest transport of these asteroid resources is not, though, from the Moon or Mars, but using the asteroids themselves, and once space transport has matured, the time to deliver resources is no longer a function. For example, the speed of oil tankers is no longer a function once the supply line is set up.

We should be using space to inspire and motivate people into science, engineering and maths.

As an observation, maybe as my observation for the short term for the United States, building up the capacity to visit beyond the Moon with significant capability including human visits, assures potential economic leadership in asteroid resources. At the Moon, excavating or inspecting around the surface and craters for minerals is, indeed, a hugely difficult task, but breakthroughs may come. Also, when we consider some who view oxygen (*from surface dust, water or ice*) as being an abundant resource on the Moon, they often don't consider the paradox of using oxygen fuel from earth to go to the Moon, to get oxygen fuel and use oxygen fuel to get back. This may not, therefore, bear a good economic return. People have also mentioned helium three from the Moon. I'm a little sceptical because, as yet, we do not have a reactor that can use helium three. My view is that there may be other isotopes on the Moon like Boron 11 which are not radioactive, and are more plentiful. These could be processed sooner, and in a less costly manner than helium three.

Looking at space tourism, my view is that we are a long way off. We may have people in orbit, but much beyond swinging by the Moon I am not sure where the economic return comes from tourism in space.

The inspiration of youth for education in the science, technology and maths disciplines is also a critical role for space. A nation like the U.S. which has reached the peak of manufacturing and trade in comparison with other areas of the world, ought to hold onto what it has as far as the inspiration of the education system goes. I am concerned that we, in the U.S., are not doing this well, as we should be using space to inspire and motivate people into science, engineering and maths. This is obviously an economic return from space.

The Survival of Humanity

Philosophically, there is also the role of space in the 'total survival' of humanity. Sooner or later an intelligent species must realise its obligation, not just to future generations, but to all the lives that been lived productively in the past. All the knowledge, progress and dedication of these many billions of lives served could be wiped out. Many would judge that an even greater loss, than the loss of future generations.

Will space teach us anything about our home environment on earth? And what is the role of private enterprise versus governments in the future of space exploration?

There have been a few emails exchanged which talk about the results of a catastrophic loss of environmental control on earth. There are many influential individuals who are quite extreme about this, I am not among them. For the satisfaction, though, of those who are concerned about the extremes of conditions that could be brought about here on earth, it seems that the immediate expenditures are not shared between those producing the adverse affects, and those spending to mitigate them. People want just those who can afford it, rather than those who produce it to spend the money. I suspect, personally, a lot of this field is political.

There may certainly be opportunities to learn from other planets about the evolving nature of natural influences which can teach us a good bit about nature here on earth, and how these influences could be detrimental in the long term to our environment. I mentioned before about mining and minerals, but I'm talking more about phenomenon such as climate change, and dust storms which would have to be coped with. The extremes of temperature, the scarcity of water, we will have to learn about how to deal with all these things on the Moon and other places. As we learn how to deal with these severe environmental conditions, in vacuum environments or limited atmospheres, and in very different gravity, we can inevitably learn how to understand and cope with changing conditions here on earth.

We must compete at the supply end of developing rockets and space craft, but co-operate in the utilisation of them.

The Role of Private Enterprise in Space Exploration

Looking at the role of private enterprise, I think we are beginning to see the areas where commercial profit making endeavours can stem; for example commercially designed space-craft and rockets which could deliver U.S. and other astronauts to the space station, in return for compensation. This provides an economic benefit which alleviates governments from getting involved in endeavours which are not directly involved in exploration. Commercial organisations are also able to get involved in refuelling, by taking fuel into space, and selling it to someone who wants to use it in low earth orbit, for lunar missions, or other purposes. This can be done by many nations who cannot afford big rockets and the total exploration package. This is something which I know is being looked at very seriously, and something which I firmly endorse as it makes the most out of in-situ [in the original place] resource utilisation (ISRU) at the Moon, other objects, and the surface of Mars. This type of commercialisation will be very important for the sustainability of these missions, and opens up viable economic routes to ship resources and the means of processing them to the Moon, Mars and other bodies to sustain settlers there for whatever reason they have arrived.

Historically, much of the progress in space exploration has come from the conflict and competition between nations. What is the role of competition in the current space exploration landscape?

The key downside to competition is duplication at the operating end which is wasteful yet inevitable as there is always more than one way of doing something. Competition at the development end, though, in creating capabilities and then sharing internationally through co-operation allows us to get the most out of competition, without suffering the waste of duplicating. In this sense, we must compete at the supply end of developing rockets and space craft, but co-operate in the utilisation of them. . . .

What are your views of the American space programme?

This has been my very challenge, realising the delay, wastefulness, and lack of productivity for the U.S to revisit the Moon. We've done it, we understand what's there pretty well, and we can continue to investigate robotically much cheaper, exerting the leadership we developed forty years ago, and in the last five years, as evidence, to assist other nations in their efforts to put their humans on the Moon for whatever inspirational or motivational reasons they may have to demonstrate to their people, and the international community, the progressive nature of their achievements.

During this process, there will inevitably be the discovery of some now unknown economic benefit which can be responded to.

For my part, I propose a two phase, two decade plan. Where at the end of the first decade we re-evaluate the overall plan of, "*clearing a pathway to settling on Mars, via the Moon of Mars as a stepping stone*". We re-evaluate at the end of one decade, and either ratchet up resources to complete that mission, have an off-ramp for asteroid or lunar development, or cancel the whole thing. Politically, if a wise pathway is charted to develop and settle on another planet, the historical significance of this is significant enough where it would not be apt to be negated by whoever is president at the Phase 2 time. I have, clearly, considered the politics involved. . . .

How can humanity share in the experience of space exploration? And what role does education play in stimulating the "spirit of adventure"?

I think we need to also publicise the availability of partial experiences and their potential to increase knowledge. The simulators of shuttle launches in Florida, for example, are getting better and better. There's also the centrifuge at Philadelphia which has a good simulation of Virgin Galactic's suborbital flights, and aircraft which fly for brief times at lunar, Martian, or zero gravity. There are also neutral buoyancy underwater experiences which could be further developed. Experiences like these could certainly also be considered educational to enhance the appreciation for the taxpayer "investments" in space exploration to help them understand why some of their money is going in that direction.

There are, though, certain prohibitions on governments spending taxpayer's money to advertise their [*government's*] activities. We need to enlighten judgement on doing that, opening more debate on vested and political interests and influences.

We live in a totally 'fogged' atmosphere where you cannot see the enormity of the stars above us.

Has your spaceflight experience changed your view on humanity and our place in the universe?

Without sounding trite, but during missions, we were busy with the items of the moment, and not too much into philosophising. In my personal life evolution, though, I don't believe that these experiences have provided more direct involvement in my life than a background. I don't believe the time of the experiences [*e.g. walking on the Moon*] and shortly thereafter had a major impact on my life, but what did have impact was dealing with my personal change in outlook as a result of dealing with, and recovering from, depression and alcoholism, which introduced the satisfying concept of a higher power in my life, totally eclipsing anything I had previously experienced including taking communion on the Moon. It caused me to take consideration, or reconsideration, of the forces, intellect, and powers of creation that have set this magnificent universe in motion including all aspects physical and spiritual.

We live in a totally 'fogged' atmosphere where you cannot see the enormity of the stars above us, and occasional meteorites, and other evidences. An individual without the intellect, wisdom or appreciation for these things will have a very restricted and narrow concept of the human intellect's place in this universe, unlike those who have given considerably more thought, including astronomers, astrophysicists, nuclear and particle physicists and some philosophers. Often these individuals (*such as [Albert] Einstein*) have been challenged because of their intellect and position, reflected only after publication of their wisdom. These individuals have had a significant impact on me as I value their intellect. I like [English theoretical physicist] Stephen Hawking, for example. I don't have to understand string-theory and all the observations, but he has a reputation around the world for not being a dreamer, but a concrete philosopher of enormous capability. I can trust his thoughts and opinions without having to say "*I believe everything he says*". I can simply grant a credit of comprehension, and go along with his views.

This can, though, get dangerous, when some high-brow scientist from an international organisation starts discussing how "*before the end of the century, oceans will rise 10ft*". I'm not sure I see credentials in these predictions based on past evidence. I (*personally*) feel I am treading on very dangerous ground as in order to get my ideas and concepts and vision for space exploration heard, I have to deal with science advisors at the very highest levels who may not quite agree with my personal thoughts on these issues, and others such as climate change.

I also feel quite free to use the hoax and UFO [unidentified flying object] people's craze and desires to further publicise my points of view and to expand knowledge on these subjects. The 'monolith on phobos' [a surface feature on Phobos, a moon of Mars], for example, will get great attention in coming years. The Canadians, and others, who have observed shadows of this topographic structure are pretty scientific in their analysis of it. But in terms of these crazes stimulating adventure, when Canadian scientists detailed their proposed robotic study of phobos and were asked, *"where are you going to land?"* their response, *"we'll go for the monolith"*.

2

The US Government Should Cut NASA Funding

Jerry DeGroot

Jerry DeGroot is a history professor at the University of St. Andrews in the United Kingdom. He is the author of several books, including Dark Side of the Moon: The Magnificent Madness of the American Lunar Quest.

Spending millions in tax money on unneeded and often unproductive National Aeronautics and Space Administration (NASA) missions is ridiculous. Funding NASA siphons money from other worthwhile, terrestrial programs such as helping the nation's poor. While NASA tries to sell its missions as patriotic endeavors, America must realize that it needs to help itself through hard economic times before investing in theoretical tomorrows.

Good sense is a terrestrial phenomenon, as the expression "down to earth" suggests. Outer space, on the other hand, provides metaphors of madness.

"Lunacy" originates from lunar, or the idea that the moon's gravitational pull adversely affects the brain. That perhaps explains the insanity that typifies American space policy.

Forget giant leaps for mankind, NASA is a machine for spending money. That fact has been driven home by the ignominious failure of the Orbiting Carbon Observatory, a $278 million package which blasted off from Vandenberg air force base on Tuesday and promptly crashed into the Pacific. The satellite, we were told, would advance the study of global warming. But NASA isn't interested in global warming; it simply realises that wearing green is a way to get government money.

While most Americans have moved on, NASA is stuck in the 1960s. That explains the desire to go to Mars, an aspiration given the seal of presidential approval in 2004. Bush's project, priced at $400 billion, was inspired by his desire to stay ahead of the Chinese in the new space race. Just as in the 1960s, the ability to make shallow gestures in space is still assumed to be an indicator of a nation's virility. During a recent radio programme, a NASA astronaut asked me how the American people might react if the next man on the moon were Chinese. I replied with a question: "why are Americans so insecure?" If the Chinese want that worthless rock, so be it."

The time has come to pull the plug on meaningless gestures in space.

Obscenely expensive manned missions mean that practical, earth-based science suffers, as does the genuinely valuable satellite research so essential to the way we live today. It is no wonder that the most articulate opposition to the Apollo missions came from Nobel scientists who objected to the way their budgets were bled in order to fund an ego trip to the moon.

Recently, Stephen Hawking has argued that we must colonise other planets to ensure mankind's long-term survival. Much as I admire Hawking, that's nonsense. The Earth is indeed doomed, but where might refugees go? Mars makes Antarctica seem like paradise. As for distant galaxies, a spaceship capable of travelling at a million miles per hour (20 times faster than Apollo) would take 4,000 years to reach the nearest star system that might theoretically be hospitable.

The time has come to pull the plug on meaningless gestures in space. An expensive mission to the moon (especially at a time of global recession) seems like lunacy when terrestrial frontiers such as disease, starvation and drought cry out for cash. Furthermore, expensive space missions add credence to fundamentalist allegations about American spiritual vacuity.

So far, Obama has sent mixed signals when it comes to space. A year before the election, he announced that a hike in education funding would be paid for by cutting the Mars mission. Then, three months later, he started courting NASA, perhaps to woo voters in Florida. By last August, he had gone full circle: expressing full support for Bush's pledge. For a man who got to the White House promising change, that sounds depressingly like 1960s logic.

While it is not Obama's habit to revere old Republicans, he would do well to study what Nixon and Eisenhower had to say about space. Nixon was the first president to catch on to NASA's trick of using past expenditure to justify future investment. As the agency argues, going to Mars will make what was spent going to the Moon a good investment. That's a clever way of endlessly spending money without ever producing anything.

But the final word goes to Eisenhower, who once vetoed Apollo. He reminded Americans that "every rocket fired signifies, in the final sense, a theft from those who hunger and are not fed, those who are cold and are not clothed."

3

The US Government Should Not Cut NASA Funding

Josh Levinger

Josh Levinger is a former graduate student at the Massachusetts Institute of Technology (MIT). His interest and work lies at the intersection of technology and activism. He now works as a lead developer at the Citizen Engagement Laboratory, an organization that seeks to use modern, digital media to give voice to underrepresented people. He wrote the following piece as a staff writer for MIT's The Tech.

The National Aeronautics and Space Administration (NASA) remains a valuable tool to help reach new planets that might host humanity if and when the Earth dies. For this monumental reason, the US government should not cut NASA's funding. The country already spends vast sums on war and defense, when it should be investing in the future of its people. To make the most of the program's dollars, the government should permit private enterprise to take part in space projects. The involvement of competitive private industry will allow NASA to focus on pioneering exploration, and—if its budget remains healthy—this eventually will lead to discoveries that will benefit the nation and humankind.

To the critics of the space program, greedy astronauts fill their pockets with our hard earned dollars and blast off into space, leaving our children with only rocket fumes for lunch. But to its proponents, space exploration represents a relatively small expenditure that brings positive real world impacts in the form of cutting edge research, crucial data on weather and climate change, thousands of jobs, and more than a few spinoff technologies. The truth is somewhere in between.

Little Is Spent on Space Exploration

Before taking the rockets versus food trade-off too seriously, let's look at some numbers objectively. The NASA [National Aeronautics and Space Administration] budget is projected to be $18 billion in 2010, half of one percent of the federal budget. To be sure, this is not pocket change. A billion here, a billion there, and soon enough you're talking about real money. But it is not outsized in comparison to other truly wasteful uses of your tax dollars. Here are but a few egregious examples: $8 billion for missile defense, $16 billion for nuclear weapons, $5 billion for foreign militaries, $12 billion for spy satellites, and $9 billion to reconstruct Iraq that has literally gone missing. You don't have to look hard to find many more examples. These are the parts of the military-industrial complex that President [Dwight D.] Eisenhower was referring to when he made the famous quote [in 1961, Eisenhower warned about the need to control the expansion of what he called the "military-industrial complex."]. Even if you consider the space program to be a waste, it's so far from our federal budget's biggest line item that a little cost-benefit analysis quickly leads you to more fertile ground.

To pretend that it's the fault of the space program that people are still starving in Africa is disingenuous at best.

I am as concerned about global poverty as anyone, and would happily put my tax dollars toward increasing non-military foreign aid. However, we have been failing that charge consistently for nearly forty years. In 1970, the advanced countries pledged 0.7 percent of their GNP [gross national product] on development assistance in front of the [United Nations] General Assembly. Today, that would be $100 billion per year, two orders of magnitude more than we are currently spending to help achieve the Millennium Development Goals [to help developing nations alleviate poverty and meet minimum health standards] by 2015.... But to pretend that it's the fault of the space program that people are still starving in Africa is disingenuous at best. We can, and should, do both.

Great Plans but No Action

Space critics are right about one thing, NASA has been rudderless for the last few years. Though charged by the [George W.] Bush administration to extend the reach of humanity back to the Moon and on to Mars, it was given no additional funding to do so. The civilian space budget has been effectively capped for the last two decades; all aeronautical, biological, and exploration related research fight for the same pool of money. Saddled with an outdated, underpowered and needlessly winged Space Shuttle, the Constellation project proposed a new launch vehicle that would return us to the glory days. However, it ended up like so many projects, behind schedule and over budget. We simply cannot develop new capability, fly the Shuttle to finish building and continue servicing the space station, and do cutting edge research without expanding the budgetary pool. Something has to go; and so, surprise, the federal government established a committee to study the problem.

The Review of Human Space Flight Plans Commission, which included the [Massachusetts Institute of Technology (MIT)] Aero/Astro department's own Dr. Edward Crawley as a member, was charged with figuring this out in June 2009. Their report last September [2009] laid down the facts on the costs of continuing our current course, and gave five options for future trajectories. They indicated that we cannot achieve our lofty goals on the current funding without sacrificing safety, and a new vision is needed. The [Barack] Obama Administration took this advice, and what they propose is something that should make even a cold libertarian heart skip a beat.

We need a backup plan, because this world won't last forever.

Cut Costs and Involve Private Enterprise

Their answer to our space budget woes? Cut fat, outsource to private companies and focus on a sustainable future. Instead of running our own nationalized shuttle service to the station, we can let Orbital Sciences and SpaceX do it for us for the low price of $5,000 per kilogram. NASA will refocus its efforts on developing next generation propulsion technologies to get us to far-flung destinations faster, cheaper, and safer than we can with the liquid hydrogen and oxygen propellants that we've used since the 1960's. Robotic precursor missions to the moon and the asteroid belt will help us work out the kinks in the navigation and descent system before we send astronauts. Federal research will push the bounds of the possible and let commercial interests fill in behind it. . . .

But these cost-containment arguments don't get to the heart of the matter: Why do we maintain a space program? It's not just for national pride. Although that was certainly a primary factor during the Cold War, it's not enough anymore to say that we need to beat the Chinese back to the moon. The reason I support the space program is a base and selfish one; we need a backup plan, because this world won't last forever. We will either continue choking it with greenhouse gases, irradiate it with our terrible weapons, or be blindsided by an asteroid. The odds are calculable, and not in our favor. [Actors] Bruce Willis and Ben Affleck can't save us from all of those threats [as they did in the 1998 movie *Armageddon*]. We need real heroes, like the engineers who toil in anonymity, designing the best damn fuel pump that they can. Heroes like the astronauts who trained on the Space Shuttle that will be cancelled before they get a chance to fly it. And heroes like children who dream big and push themselves to study science and engineering even when the going gets tough.

I, for one, am glad that people still stare up at the stars, even if things still need work here on Earth. How else will we get to the future that we all deserve?

4

America Needs Space Exploration to Maintain Its Vision of Itself

Bob Deutsch

Bob Deutsch is a cognitive anthropologist and founder of the firm Brain Sells, a strategic branding and communications consultancy based in Boston, Massachusetts.

The Founding Fathers established the country on the idea of liberty combined with creativity, which allows for both caring for practical concerns and looking beyond the needs of the moment. The current economic downturn and global situation suggest that Americans should focus solely on the numbers for improving budgets and analysis of metrics. Instead, Americans should focus on the unknown as a means of fostering creativity and providing deeper insights than those produced by reliance on numerical measurement alone. America has a heritage of exploring new frontiers, and the space program provides that new frontier and the means of escaping beyond the now.

Before compromise budgetary legislation was passed earlier this fall [2010], Pres. Barack Obama had called for grounding NASA's [National Aeronautical and Space Administration] space program that would have taken astronauts back to the moon and beyond. In seeking cheaper, faster ways of keeping the U.S. in an exploratory orbit, budgetary issues should not be the only consideration. The country needs a robust space program if we are to realize fully our psychic potential as explorer and player in an ever-expanding frontier.

Our nation finds itself on a treadmill, moving in a simple, two-dimensional motion, burning calories but not exactly sure where it is going. What is required for our national health is a balanced complexity of motion (and its attendant experience) that allows one to feel simultaneously "here" at the center and "out there" at the boundaries. Now, more than ever, in the midst of an economic downturn, and facing a future felt to be receding, Americans need to exist on two planes: the mundane and the mythic.

Curtailing the space program is a bad idea.

Never Constrained by the Status Quo

Our Founding Fathers established the U.S. as an idea, not an ideal. The idea was of liberty and creativity combined, never to be constrained by the status quo. The vision of George Washington, Thomas Jefferson, Benjamin Franklin, and their band of brothers was rooted in the pragmatics of daily life and cast beyond the pale, into the boundless frontier.

The early 21st century certainly is a different time than the late 18th but underneath the momentary talk, Americans maintain a deep appreciation and need for what this country represents. For instance, in the mid 1990s, I was talking to citizens concerning the proposed luxury car tariff against Japanese automakers, a hot topic at the time. In one discussion, a young woman, a native of Detroit [Michigan] said, "For a couple of generations, members of my family have worked here in the American auto industry. I'm scared about the Japanese competition, but I think tariffs are a bad idea." I asked her why. Upon hearing her response, the earth seemed to shake under the feet of the 11 people in that room, including me. She uttered just three short but profound, sentences: "America is a good idea. The idea is freedom. Tariffs are a bad idea." The U.S.'s intrinsic nature is to be open and exploratory. That particularly is a good idea now. Curtailing the space program is a bad idea.

The thinking of this one woman reflects the essence of the relationship that liberty has to creativity—breaking out of routine and expected patterns and going beyond a top-of-mind, business-as-usual, short-term horizon. What is required to live in this frame of mind is having an idea of yourself as one who stands above the press of the moment. Such a mindset allows a practical rootedness in one's authenticity and a "thinking up" that is optimistic and innovative. However, many Americans today feel boxed in by fear. Since words like "ponzi" and "derivatives" have entered their lexicon, they have been living in a question mark—heads down and shoulders hunched in a protective posture.

Space exploration can help the nation renew its national mythology.

Why the United States Must Explore Space

This is exactly why the U.S. must explore space. We need a program to reimagine a frontier that will allow us to open up this hunkered-down existence. The arguments against it are coldly logical and sometimes all too true. It is too expensive; there is little immediate benefit. The problem with those contentions is that they are blind to the human need to address the cosmic questions of life: Who are we? How are we unique? Why are we here? How did it all begin?

The U.S. has been a place—and should remain one—in which these types of questions are asked. Admittedly, these "big" questions may never be answered satisfactorily but during the search, exploration itself becomes the driving force—our nation in search of the frontier, spatially and experientially. To make this happen, we need a sense of place that includes what is known and what is not, what is possible and what lies beyond our capabilities. Without such urgency of mind, the time frame of our intentions becomes shorter and our motives smaller-minded.

As an anthropologist who traded his backpack and quinine tablets for a Hartmann two-suiter and Dramamine, I have lived among preliterate tribes who have no information technologies, malls, nor media. Their world falls far short of utopia. Life is hard in the primeval forest but what these weathered-skinned people do have is a general comfort level borne out of an assumed connectedness to their cosmos. Their mythology is rock-solid and enables them to carry on. The U.S. now finds itself "between mythologies." We are not what we once were (mostly because the world changed on us), and we do not yet know what we will become. Where once we had enough resources and weight to overcome any obstacle, we now face a world full of perplexing challenges. Space exploration can help the nation renew its national mythology.

How the country acts during this stage of identity transition will define what it becomes at the conclusion of this national rite de passage. To again take its place as a leader among nations and a beacon for all, the U.S. must remain open, imaginative, and creative; on the intellectual offense; and always exploring. It cannot succumb to the moment's impulse to recoil or resist. Space exploration provides a higher point of view from which to see ourselves. Such a vantage point paves the way for an openness of mind and a generosity of spirit.

We must go beyond metrics and groupthink. Data points are not people. Spreadsheets are not artful. To do something artfully requires a dynamic mix of imagination and understanding to see how the world might work. This is not a matter of being correct but of provoking a self-referring reverie in people that elicits an expanded idea of themselves and their place in the world. As a result they see anew.

This approach, of course, runs counter to today's government and corporate metric-mania that produces a diminished capacity to conceive bold and innovative visions and strategies. Numbers, budgetary or otherwise, can provide a means for measurement but cannot "embody" or suggest meaningful insights into the human experience. Yet such insights are the base coin of national and commercial success.

The U.S. was founded on the idea of never accepting the status quo and always exploring further.

Creativity

Creativity calls for a focused subjectivity and the capacity to doubt: an ability to focus on something long enough and deep enough to conjure possibilities not seen in the manifest and immediate moment along with a healthy acknowledgement that not everything is known. The unknown is fertile soil from which a world of wonders can be cultivated. Here, the plodding of facts and data is circumvented in a nonlinear, symbolic, not wholly rational way. In this maneuver, the mind plays a cognitive trick on itself by creating metaphor. "I will call what I do not know by the name of something that I do know." Suddenly, you become free to explore conceptually. You are released from the rut of the "now" and the already-known. Through this mental leapfrog, the creative impulse extrapolates into unknown scenarios. It moves from the past to instigate an inkling that lays the basis for the beginning of a new narrative, to a springboard that weaves a web of new patterns and associations, to an insinuation of the future as projected in metaphor. This process produces, from the outside-objective point of view, what can be perceived as seemingly off-topic meanderings, but nothing is further from the truth.

What is in operation is a kind of playfulness with ideas that is essential for creativity. This toying around contains a bunch of no's, as in no pretense, analyzing (yet), doubts, pressure to conform, restrictions, and, perhaps most important of all, judgment. Those who are playfully creative possess a curiosity given backbone by their expectation that they will find what they seek even though they do not know what it is they seek (often a statement of fact in space exploration).

In this special state of mental weightlessness, all inhabitants are joined by a belief in a beautiful human quality, directed serendipity: I have a plan because the plan allows me to begin to move forward and, in doing so, I learn about myself. You sort of go down a path and things evolve. By adapting and adjusting to randomness, you shape, but do not control, your endpoint. Yet you define your endpoint by your own reaction to it—ah, ha! I like this. This is for me. This is me.

However, in sharp contrast many more Americans today are losing hope in the ties that bind hard work to success. Many see the future as "closing." This mentality foreshortens their vision of self, others, and the world. This orientation, about almost everything, is defensive. Listen to the tone: money makes the world go around; now I have less money and hope—or, I feel better when I see someone worse off than me; I have to fight for everything, and I don't have a lot. In other words, what's the point?

The U.S. was founded on the idea of never accepting the status quo and always exploring further. It is our national heritage, and it is not nice to fool with a nation's nature. NASA's manned space program, particularly in times of uncertainty and fear, can help remind each American what it means to look up and open up—to have an idea of "you" that has a little elbow room.

Only the space program can provide a national effervescence that can give people that boost necessary to investigate their own essence, to write their own story. Manned exploration of space instigates a reverie to help people feel they are more fully alive and participating in a quest beyond the mundane. The very idea of breaking past Earth's pull can help keep people from being inundated by the contingency of any moment.

When thinking about one's own life, there is a sense of freedom in keeping the mind's eye oriented to the "out there, beyond the boundaries" of daily existence. To hold dear this attitude, it helps to realize that astronauts, space stations, the Hubble telescope, etc. represent—and are a reflection of—who we are. More than any other idea the NASA program allows people to experience the reality that we are but a small speck amidst the immensity of intergalactic space and that we are one with it. To partake daily of this mystery, to wonder, to feel and never flat-line emotionally, lies at the core of the idea of manned space exploration. It is there to help each American—in the context of his or her own life—soar and explore.

International and Private Competition Benefits Space Exploration

James Oberg

A former National Aeronautics and Space Administration (NASA) scientist, James Oberg is now a promoter of space exploration and a space consultant for NBC News. He has written ten books and numerous articles on space flight, including The New Race for Space, *a detailed study of the prospects for greater cooperation between the US and Russian space programs.*

In the coming decade, many nations and private firms will provide a boost to space exploration by sending space probes and planetary explorers into the solar system. Between 2011 and 2015, Russia, China, Japan, the United States, and the European Space Agency all will be investing in and conducting robotic missions to Mars and the Moon while also planning potential launches to investigate the Sun, Jupiter, Venus, and other extraterrestrial bodies before the end of the decade. Private industry also has taken advantage of an international contest to send a lunar rover to the Moon by 2013, hoping to prove that space missions might be accomplished relatively cheaply and without national funding. This flurry of international and private competition suggests that space exploration is proceeding steadily and will likely include manned, deep-space missions sometime in the foreseeable future.

After half a century of increasingly far-reaching robotic exploration of the solar system, we have moved to a higher level of activity. No longer are missions episodic, planetary visits brief, or trajectories one way. The time is near when probes will observe all worlds of interest almost constantly. And the first "return to sender" missions are already in the textbooks, with even more ambitious round-trip flights in sight.

On the other hand, the forecast resumption of human flight to the Moon and the possibility of new forms of an international "Moon race" have vanished. This will be another decade without human flight beyond low Earth orbit, but with any luck it will be the last in history.

Previewing the next decade's fleet of spacecraft is a challenge because firm plans and reliable financing are hard to predict. And with the scope of destinations so wide, and the cast of players so grand, no matter how impressive a roster we outline today, by 2020 we can be sure a good number of surprises will await us.

Right now, various active probes . . . are on interplanetary trajectories or already on the surfaces of other worlds.

Missions Already in Flight

Any forecast of interplanetary exploration in the 2010s must begin with the probes currently in flight, whether en route to distant worlds, already there, or on post-primary-mission extensions. Next, the new crop of spacecraft, many of them delayed for years, will supplement that fleet. The middle of the decade will see two new launch surges sown: more ambitious government-sponsored missions, and a ragtag collection of private Moon missions seeking glory and cash rewards. The second half of the decade will host an even wider assortment of lunar and planetary spacecraft that will pioneer new trails, expand old ones, and extend human senses into new environments.

Right now, various active probes—most of them American, the rest European and Asian—are on interplanetary trajectories or already on the surfaces of other worlds. It's striking just how complete existing coverage is, presaging a permanent robotic presence across most of the solar system. Just running down the list of planets and other targets, we have:

Mercury: The MESSENGER probe is en route to arrive March 18 [2011].

Venus: Europe's Venus Express and Japan's Akatsuki probes are in orbit studying the atmosphere.

The Moon: NASA's [National Aeronautics and Space Administration] Lunar Reconnaissance Orbiter (LRO) still maps the Moon from orbit along with the second Chinese orbiter, Chang'e 2, and two veteran solar wind monitors are settling into stable orbit near the Earth-Moon system.

Mars: Three orbiters (Mars Odyssey, Mars Reconnaissance Orbiter, and Mars Express) and one surviving rover (Opportunity) just keep beating the odds on the Red Planet.

The asteroid belt: Dawn is already there, still traveling to asteroid 4 Vesta, which it will study for a year before departing for the dwarf planet 1 Ceres.

Jupiter: The king of planets is temporarily unvisited.

Saturn: The Cassini "Extended-Extended Mission" roams the entire system's moons and rings.

Uranus and Neptune: The ice giants are currently off the target list.

Pluto: New Horizons hibernates while coasting onward, finally arriving in July 2015; afterward, astronomers hope to nudge the probe's path toward farther Kuiper Belt objects.

Not all flight paths are so cut and dried. This past summer [2010], the European probe Rosetta voyaged through the asteroid belt, and it will enter deep-space hibernation in May, arriving at its cometary target 3 years later. Its Philae lander is scheduled to alight on 67P/Churyumov-Gerasimenko in November 2014. The main probe will orbit the object and continue studying it for years.

Even if no further probes launch for years, the existing fleet could fill the decade with discoveries.

And, unforgettably, the Voyager 1 and 2 spacecraft are still going strong as they measure the edges of the solar system and the environment of interstellar space.

Closer to home, several smaller spacecraft that long ago fulfilled their primary missions are still operating, following redirection to new targets. In November 2010, the Deep Impact probe, as part of its EPOXI mission, passed Comet 103P/Hartley more than 5 years after it deployed an impactor into the comet 9P/Tempel (also known as Tempel 1); it now awaits further orders. Tempel 1 is also the next stop for the Stardust spacecraft, which successfully collected cometary dust and dropped the sample back on Earth in 2006. The flyby is scheduled for February 14, 2011—with possible targets beyond. And the revolutionary Ikaros solar sail, a Japanese experimental craft, launched in May 2010, piggy-backing on Akatsuki; it's destined for a years-long sunlight-fueled journey through the inner solar system, ultimately toward the Sun.

Even if no further probes launch for years, the existing fleet could fill the decade with discoveries.

Near-Term Launches from Around the Globe

Besides the missions already in space, there's plenty more to come. The most newsworthy development of 2011 ought to be when Russia finally resumes its historic role as a major player in space exploration, 2 decades after the collapse of the Soviet Union and its space ambitions.

A handful of modest missions will keep the launch pads warm for most of the year. NASA's next Jupiter orbiter, Juno, is slated for launch in August on a 5-year trip to its target. Using new super-efficient solar panels (a first for an outer solar system probe), Juno will settle into a wide-ranging polar orbit to study the planet's atmosphere and magnetosphere for at least 1 year.

In September, NASA will launch the Gravity Recovery and Interior Laboratory (GRAIL) mission, in which twin spacecraft will fly in tandem orbits around the Moon for 3 months to measure its gravity field with unprecedented precision. And the success this past summer of Japan's asteroid-sampling Hayabusa spacecraft will probably keep the orbiting space rocks as a viable destination as well, with a possible second mission occurring in 2014. If launched that year, the mission's target would be asteroid 1999 JU3, a C-type carbon-rich body.

Near the end of the year, two major missions will take advantage of the 2011 Mars launch window. This brief period opens up every 2.2 years when the orbits of Earth and Mars "line up" to minimize the energy required for a spacecraft to reach the Red Planet. One mission plans to bring a soil sample back to Earth's laboratories, and the other hopes to send a world-class biology lab to martian soil. Both missions were delayed from the previous launch window, and both have a much better chance of succeeding because of that delay.

The first, Russia's Fobos-Grunt (meaning "Phobos Soil") will end a quarter-century absence of the world's space pioneer by obtaining and returning samples from the martian moon Phobos. It will also deploy Yinghuo-1, a Chinese Mars orbiter hitching a ride. After a big push to make the 2009 window, Russian space officials decided their spacecraft wasn't ready for such an ambitious mission. In the time since, they've entirely rebuilt its soil retrieval hardware and gave it other reliability improvements.

The second mission is NASA's Mars Science Laboratory rover, also known as Curiosity, which will seek signs of martian biochemistry (or even life) on its years-long trek across the surface. Curiosity's science gear is some 10 times heavier than the current rovers, and it has 4 times their electrical power (the nuclear power system could last more than 14 years). In its planned 2-year lifetime, it should traverse about 12 miles (19 kilometers), approximately the same range Opportunity has achieved in 7 years.

National and Private Interests in Lunar Exploration

Lunar missions dominate the current plans for 2012 and beyond. The first Russian lunar probe in 40 years, Luna-Glob 1 (meaning "Lunar Globe"), should launch next year to study seismic properties of the Moon from orbit. Also, the Indian Chandrayaan-II lunar mission is scheduled to launch in 2013, carrying a Russian-built lander called Luna-Resurs ("Lunar Resource") that, in turn, will carry a Russian-built rover. And China's Chang'e 3 will attempt that country's first lunar landing and rover deployment, with the Japanese following suit in 2015 with their SELENE-2 combination lunar orbiter, lander, and rover.

Lunar missions dominate the current plans for 2012 and beyond.

The surge in lunar exploration reflects the calculated decisions of national space agencies, but a second source of lunar robot missions will follow soon afterward. The private X Prize Foundation has organized the Google Lunar X Prize, which offers a $20 million prize and multimillion-dollar bonuses for successful Moon robots. An array of private groups has stepped forward and announced plans to participate.

There are more than 20 teams, with headquarters in more than 10 countries, according to Will Pomerantz, senior director of space prizes. "Most are multinational, and individual team members are working in 65 different countries."

"We have a lot more teams, and better teams, than we expected," Pomerantz says. The winning team will be the first to land a robot on the Moon that travels more than 1,640 feet (500 meters) and returns high-definition images and video. But to win the full prize, the team must accomplish this before 2013, when the $20 million decreases to $15 million, with the contest expiring in 2015.

Private Firms Expect to Lower Mission Costs

But Pomerantz doesn't expect the private Moon missions to end once the prizes are won. "We're trying to prime the pump" for ongoing activities, he says, meaning at least several flights per year for the rest of the decade. Bare bones and cheap private missions could open "all kinds of markets," whose customers might include national space agencies, private corporations, university alliances, and even the entertainment industry. Small robots could scout landing sites, provide package delivery services, obtain (and sell) imagery, and provide other scientific measurements, as well as, of course, unpredictable applications. Hardware developed for the different teams could establish permanent lunar navigation and communications services, making other missions much less technologically challenging.

Participation isn't cheap. Historically, serious contenders in aviation prizes over the past century spent between 2 and 5 times as much money as they had a chance of winning—but they expected to come out ahead with later commercialization opportunities. Although a few teams think they can win and spend less than the prize value, Pomerantz says, "The majority of the teams are looking at spending $50 to $75 million, including launch costs. This remains substantially below the costs of more-sophisticated government missions."

Whether private Moon robots will be able to reach acceptable levels of reliability and timeliness is an open question. But the answer might dominate Moon mission traffic by the end of this decade.

NASA is also encouraging deployment of commercial navigation and communication services in lunar orbit. In mid-2010, the agency announced plans to purchase specific data resulting from private efforts to test and verify vehicle capabilities through demonstrations of small robotic landers. Called the Innovative Lunar Demonstrations Data project, it will provide grants with the option of purchasing resulting engineering data for Earth-to-Moon flight system capabilities and test technologies.

Plans for Other Nationally Funded Missions

Despite the rise of privately funded missions to the Moon and potentially other destinations as well, big government space agencies still plan on flying sophisticated interplanetary probes in the second half of this decade.

Russia has decided to return to the martian surface in 2016 for the first time since a series of bitter failures in the early 1970s. MetNet (typically translated "Mars Weather Net") involves deploying a number of small sensors—some resting on the surface and others penetrating several meters underground—for seismic and environmental studies. At the same time, two joint European Space Agency (ESA) and NASA missions will make up the ExoMars program, which will study the potential biological conditions on Mars. The first consists of an orbiter delivering a static meteorological station, launched in 2016; the other mission, launching in 2018, will land two rovers together on the surface, the first time two vehicles will be active in such a close area.

Several countries are also planning missions to take probes closer than ever to the Sun. NASA's Solar Probe Plus—the first mission into the solar atmosphere—will use technology developed for the MESSENGER probe visiting Mercury and aims to launch in 2015. An ESA mission called Solar Orbiter would also launch in 2015 to study the Sun's hard-to-observe polar regions. Russia intends to get in on the fun with its planned Interheliozond mission in the late 2010s, involving a close solar pass within 30 solar radii, or about 13 million miles (21 million km).

Details are naturally sketchiest for the end of the decade, but already plans for some intriguing missions are under way. Russia anticipates launching a Venus probe, built in partnership with France, called Venera-D. Technicians designed the lander to operate for several days, and it will deploy two small rovers. Japan hopes to launch a spacecraft toward Jupiter, possibly propelled via solar sail, as with Ikaros. And the NASA/ESA Europa Jupiter System Mission (EJSM) might launch in 2020 to follow up on the major discoveries of the Galileo and Voyager missions at Europa, especially its likely moon-wide subsurface ocean. On the way to Europa, EJSM will tour the jovian system and make routine and frequent observations of Jupiter and its other satellites. Of course, these are all only possibilities at this time.

Despite the rise of privately funded missions to the Moon and potentially other destinations as well, big government space agencies still plan on flying sophisticated interplanetary probes in the second half of this decade.

Grander Dreams on the Horizon

The next 10 years will witness more than a mere expansion of interplanetary traffic. The very nature of the traffic will change, as permanence and round-trip missions come to dominate. What now seems surprising—having probes headed toward or already at almost every target of interest in the solar system—will become the norm by 2020.

As hardware improves for missions before 2020, one can expect that currently inconceivable missions will, in turn, receive funding and eventually see their launch dates. Most fantastically of all, perhaps this decade's missions may prove precursors for the arrival of human travelers on the deep-space stage.

6

International Cooperation Benefits Space Exploration

Scott Horowitz

A former space shuttle astronaut, Scott Horowitz served as the associate administrator for the Exploration Systems Mission Directorate at the National Aeronautics and Space Administration (NASA) headquarters in Washington, D.C., from 2005 until 2007.

Although the United States and the Soviet Union were the first nations to send manned and unmanned craft into space during the competitive "space race," of the mid-twentieth century, exploration of the stars and the planets has since become an international venture. From the cooperative US-Soviet Apollo-Soyuz mission of the 1970s to the Space Shuttle-Mir joint program of the 1990s, the two superpowers have demonstrated a willingness to work together. And in the late twentieth and early twenty-first centuries, other nations have initiated collaborative missions to further space exploration. Today astronauts come from many nations, and eighty countries have contributed technology as well as personnel to space missions. This spirit of unity will help all nations recognize that the shared benefits of space exploration can serve all of humankind.

Over the past 50 years, humans have made significant strides in space exploration. What rises above the specific details of these accomplishments, however, is the worldwide

Scott Horowitz, "Nations in Space," *eJournal USA: Science: Global Issues*, vol. 11, no. 3, October 2006, pp. 5–8. Copyright © 2006 by U.S. Department of State, Bureau of International Information Programs. Reproduced by permission.

effort and cooperation that made them possible. I believe that the growing spirit of collaboration, linked to the growing number of nations and organizations involved in space and the increasing scope of global space activity, will provide the framework required for even greater accomplishments.

The number of countries involved in space exploration has grown from a small, select group beginning in the 1950s to more than 80 nations that today have organized efforts to use space exploration to benefit their societies. The future of space exploration will be grounded in such international involvement and, more importantly, in collaboration among nations to benefit people everywhere.

As the magnitude of space exploration increases, so does international, collaborative effort.

Amazing Progress in Space Exploration

The history of space exploration is rich. In 1609, people began to explore the heavens visually thanks to improvements that Italian astronomer Galileo Galilei made to the telescope. Credited as the first to use the telescope for astronomical purposes, Galileo made it possible to observe mountains and craters on the moon's surface.

In such beginnings, the dream of lunar and planetary exploration was born. Now, 12 men have walked on the moon, and a wide range of unmanned missions to the moon and several planets have been completed. In just the past 10 years, 150 planets have been discovered beyond our solar system. Closer to home, world citizens have reaped enormous benefits from space exploration through satellites that support communication, navigation, weather observation, and other remote-sensing disciplines. Space-related technologies and scientific knowledge have contributed to high-performance computing and robotics, scratch-resistant eyeglass lenses, breast cancer imaging, and much more.

For the near future, even more ambitious space exploration plans are in development. With completion of the New Horizons mission, the first spacecraft to visit the dwarf planet Pluto and its moon Charon in 2016–2017, the world's spacefaring nations will have sent robotic spacecraft to all the planets of our solar system. No later than 2020, we expect humans to once again walk on the moon. As the magnitude of space exploration increases, so does international, collaborative effort.

The United States and the Soviet Union Link Projects

A good example of early space cooperation is the study of Halley's comet during its approach to the sun in 1986. Five years earlier, in 1981, the space agencies of the Soviet Union, Japan, Europe, and the United States formed the Inter-Agency Consultative Group (IACG) to informally coordinate matters related to the space missions being planned to observe the comet. In 1986, five spacecraft from these nations rendezvoused with Halley's comet. The vital information exchanged as a result of IACG collaboration was invaluable in studying the comet.

In human spaceflight, international collaboration has grown from the seeds of early programs such as *Skylab*, the Apollo-Soyuz Test Project, and the Space Shuttle-*Mir* Joint Program, to the current International Space Station effort, one of the most incredible engineering accomplishments in history.

The Apollo-Soyuz Test Project, July 15–24, 1975, was the first international manned space flight. The mission was designed to test rendezvous and docking systems compatibility for American and Soviet spacecraft and open the way for international space rescue and future joint manned flights.

The Space Shuttle-*Mir* Joint Program, February 1994 to June 1998, went well beyond the scope of earlier collaborative programs, encompassing 11 space shuttle flights and seven U.S. astronaut residencies, called increments, on the Russian space station *Mir*. Space shuttles also conducted crew exchanges and delivered supplies and equipment. Shuttle-*Mir* showed that space exploration no longer had to be defined as a competition between nations and helped Americans and Russians develop the expertise to build and maintain the International Space Station.

Collective Efforts Benefit All

The International Space Station is the largest international science collaboration in space today. The United States, Japan, Canada, Russia, and 11 countries represented by the European Space Agency have come together to build and inhabit the station. Through the science performed there, these nations seek to improve life on Earth and pave the way for future space exploration. The space station partnership has illustrated its strength and commitment with its perseverance through various strains, including aftershocks from the loss of the U.S. space shuttle *Columbia* in 2003.

Such cooperative endeavors serve as inspiration for the future. When great nations seek great endeavors, they find more success with allies and partners. Space exploration is the great endeavor of our time.

As much as we can take pride in our past accomplishments, the dawn of a new space age lies ahead. In a relatively short amount of time, I believe the people of Earth will look through their telescopes at the moon to see evidence of human and robotic exploration activity benefiting people everywhere.

They may see a surface research station, manned by an international crew that is working to obtain useful resources from the lunar regolith—a layer of loose rock resting on bedrock—as part of an effort to enable crews to live more independently of Earth. Antennas may be deployed on the far side of the moon that can be linked in phase to form the largest radio telescope ever built, free from the interference of radio noise from Earth. Other astronauts may be geological explorers, looking for clues to the origins of the Earth-moon system and life itself. While these activities are taking place, still others may be readying a 500-ton spaceship for humankind's first voyage to Mars.

When great nations seek great endeavors, they find more success with allies and partners.

Exploring the Moon

Already, many nations have initiated lunar exploration efforts. The European Space Agency's Small Mission for Advanced Research in Technology orbited the moon in 2004. Over the next several years, other spacecraft will follow, including the Selenological and Engineering Explorer from Japan, *Chandrayan* from India, *Chang'e* from China, and the Lunar Reconnaissance Orbiter and its secondary payload, the Lunar Crater Observation and Sensing Satellite, from the United States. Each mission has some degree of international collaboration.

In 2006, the world's spacefaring nations began discussing how they will work together to advance scientific, economic, and exploration progress on the moon. This effort begins now, with the planning and implementation of precursor robotic missions. These interactions are the seeds of future collaborative efforts.

NASA [National Aeronautics and Space Administration] is compiling input from various communities, including international space agencies, to generate a global strategy of lunar exploration objectives. NASA presented this strategy at its Next Generation Exploration Conference, a gathering of emerging global space leaders, in August 2006.

The First Step in Broader, Cooperative Ventures

As spacefaring nations come together to develop a vision of common and unique interests in the moon, we lay the groundwork for a momentous leap forward in space exploration. Some among us may see the moon as an end in itself, a unique location from which to investigate the processes that formed our solar system and a nearby location where self-sufficient human settlements may lay the groundwork for people to live and work on other worlds. Others may see the moon as a test site for technologies and operational techniques that will someday apply to the human exploration of Mars and other destinations. Still others may view the moon as an incredible resource that may help us solve energy and other problems here on Earth. Lunar exploration that is sustainable over the long term will require the efforts of all of us, with our many views of the role of the moon in human exploration and development.

As spacefaring nations come together ... we lay the groundwork for a momentous leap forward in space exploration.

When I was an astronaut, I experienced firsthand the benefits of international cooperation in space exploration. I believe in the great value of space exploration for people throughout the world. Although humankind's first steps onto another world were taken by a dozen early explorers from America, it will take all of our nations, working together, to accomplish the great endeavor of space exploration that lies before us and to enable future generations of explorers to do the things we can only imagine today.

7

Commercialization of Space Travel Will Benefit Space Exploration

Leonard David

Former editor-in-chief of the National Space Society's Ad Astra *and* Space World *magazines, Leonard David has been reporting on the space industry for more than five decades.*

The private sector has entered the space flight arena with passenger projects and technological developments. The government already has allowed private firms to participate in space missions, but it must continue to encourage this burgeoning market. Commercial firms and private investors have great sources of wealth that the National Aeronautics and Space Administration (NASA) can use to take the pressure off government funding, while NASA has the expertise and track record to provide safety control and engender public trust. Working together, the two sectors can and will achieve more successes in the near future than each could working apart.

It's been a wild and crazy ride in space since the first decade of the 21st century began, but as it nears its close the realm of commercial space travel has taken one giant leap into reality. Now, commercial space is on a growth-curve, with a whirlwind of large and small companies ready to offer a variety of skills.

There is growing recognition of this fact, evidenced by the recent "Review of U.S. Human Space Flight Plans Committee"—a report that spotlighted the commercial space industry, advising NASA [National Aeronautics and Space Administration] to encourage and use more commercial space services to support future human space missions.

Even so, the coming year is shaping up like a space-based game of "Truth or Dare".

Some see a tradition-breaking paradigm in the offing, one that increases the reliance on the private sector for space tasks. Others are not sure, envisioning risky hand-shakes with firms that offer little in the way of track record.

Commercial Exploits in Space Exploration

There's a roster of big moments in commercial spaceflight throughout the last decade.

Over the last 10 years, Space Adventures, headquartered in Vienna, Va., has organized flights for well-heeled clients to the International Space Station. That highfalutin enterprise was kick-started in 2001 by the flight of Dennis Tito—billed by the company as the world's first private space explorer. Since then, six other wealthy space enthusiasts (most recently, Canadian billionaire and Cirque du Soleil founder Guy Laliberte) have paid up to $35 million for similar treks.

Then there were the first private suborbital space treks via SpaceShipOne, bankrolled by the Microsoft-made billionaire, Paul Allen. Aerospace maverick, Burt Rutan and his Scaled Composites squad pushed the frontiers of private space travel. In doing so, they won in 2004 the $10 million Ansari X Prize for commercial spaceflight. That momentum is resident in the rollout of SpaceShipTwo earlier this month [December 2009]—a six-passenger, two-pilot suborbital craft backed and operated by Sir Richard Branson's Virgin Galactic.

Toss in for good measure, two privately funded prototype expandable space habitats that now circle the Earth. They were orbited courtesy of motel and construction mogul, Robert Bigelow, aided by his Bigelow Aerospace team in Las Vegas,

Nev. Those Genesis 1 and Genesis 2 vessels launched in 2006 and 2007, respectively, are precursors to ever-larger modules and space facilities the firm plans to orbit in future years.

Space Exploration Technologies Corporation (SpaceX) of Hawthorne, Calif., was self-financed in 2002 by PayPal co-founder, Elon Musk. Over the last eight years, the company—and its now 800 SpaceX team members—has forged ahead with development of its Falcon 1 and Falcon 9 boosters, as well as its Dragon spacecraft built to satisfy NASA's Commercial Orbital Transportation Services (COTS) program objectives.

For true space grit, several smaller space firms have blasted their way to the forefront, such as XCOR Aerospace of Mojave, Calif. Kudos were deservedly earned by Masten Space Systems, also of Mojave, as well as Armadillo Aerospace based in Rockwall, Texas. This dynamic duo pocketed prize money by competing in the NASA-backed, Northrop Grumman-sponsored Lunar Lander Challenge. The two winning companies qualified for cash prizes—managed by the X Prize Foundation—by building and flying vertical-takeoff-and-landing vehicles that hovered for up to 180 seconds, translated horizontally, landed under rocket power, and repeated the feat in two hours.

Interaction Between Government and Private Interests

So there you have it: Development of privately financed suborbital vehicles; increasing numbers of "pay-per-view" space travelers; commercial boosters and spacecraft for carriage of cargo and humans to and from Earth orbit.

Admittedly, this is a shortlist of milestones—but the trends are clear.

Nevertheless, all this "work-in-progress" remains just that. For several experts, major hurdles remain.

At first blush, it would seem there's been a shift toward the federal government embracing commercial spaceflight as a "crutch" to deal with an ailing NASA—a space agency viewed by some as in bureaucratic freefall and in need of transitioning to a more commercial-friendly realization.

"It's a complex issue ranging from legal to very practical issues," one that is an international issue as well as a domestic one, suggested Henry Hertzfeld, Research Professor of Space Policy and International Affairs and Adjunct Professor of Law at the George Washington University in Washington, D.C.

Hertzfeld said a central question is this: Is the government's embrace of commercial space a budget issue or a "hope and prayer?" Also, another up front question needs resolution—is there really a good definition of commercial space?

"To me, the bottom line test focuses not on commercial or government but on who is really taking the risks, both financial and technical," Hertzfeld said. "And, if you put almost all of the 'commercial' partnerships to that test," he continued, "I think you will find the government is footing the risk in most cases, which means they will also end up paying for it eventually in one way or another."

The Advantage of Deep Pockets

One of the most fascinating developments of the last decade, commercial space has become "the cool kids' table" for a surprising number of very wealthy individuals, observed Carissa Christensen, Managing Partner of the Tauri Group in Alexandria, Va.

"Their personal commitment has enabled firms developing commercial space vehicles to weather recent economic storms, either through their own deep pockets or because their credibility as global entrepreneurs has attracted other investors," Christensen told SPACE.com.

Christensen stressed that balance is important in viewing the relationship between government and industry in commercial space.

Commercial space has become "the cool kids' table" for a surprising number of very wealthy individuals.

"Many areas of government reliance on industry are sensible and should be part of a durable national strategy," Christensen added. For example, government funding of research and development, purchases of commercial satellite services, and contracting for launches; hardware, and engineering support.

"There is a baby/bathwater thing to be careful of here," Christensen said.

What about major obstacles ahead for commercial spaceflight?

"The biggest one is generating enough revenue to create a durable, viable industry. The challenges the industry faces are business challenges, far more than technology challenges" Christensen responded. "Just as a reminder," she added, "Concorde shut its door, and that wasn't because supersonic flight was too much of a technology challenge—it was because, ultimately, the business case didn't close."

All that being said, Christensen's view of today's private sector landscape, and drawing upon her background of working in commercial space since 1987: "This is by far the most thrilling period I have seen!"

Creating Opportunities for Cooperation

"What we are seeing in NASA is not a tidal shift in its relationship to the private sector—but a small step toward a practical approach to space," said Rick Tumlinson, co-founder of the Space Frontier Foundation and a devoted NewSpace activist and agitator. "This is occurring because of years of pressure, repeated demonstrations of the private sector's ability to perform, financial necessity and the gradual ascension of those who, 'get it' within the ranks of the space agency."

Tumlinson said that if NASA is to ever move beyond low Earth orbit and get back to the sorts of exploration missions it did in the glory days of Apollo, "it must hand off operations to the people."

Co-operation in opening the frontier is the new key to success for all, Tumlinson said: NASA gets lower costs and the ability to focus on its mission of exploration while commercial space gets the funding and early catalytic markets it needs to grow and become vital on its own.

It's time for the commercial space sector to walk the walk, not just talk the talk.

"Everyone wins—especially the people who pay for it all, as they get an open and expanding new frontier in space," Tumlinson stated.

It's time for the commercial space sector to walk the walk, not just talk the talk.

That's the attitude of John Logsdon, a distinguished space policy guru. He's Professor Emeritus of Political Science and International Affairs at the Space Policy Institute within the Elliott School of International Affairs at the George Washington University in Washington, D.C.

"It seems to me that the coming decade will be for the commercial sector the time to provide results in place of rhetoric," Logsdon advised. Between contracting for commercial cargo and commercial crew to the International Space Station, he said, NASA is providing the kind of guaranteed market the commercial sector has said it needs to get over the financial hump.

"Now is the time for the commercial sector to deliver on its promises," Logsdon said. "A government-commercial partnership can provide the stimulus for much more rapid space development than we have seen in recent years. Then 'purely' commercial activities such as space tourism can follow," he concluded.

8

Space Exploration Is Driven by a Need to Expand Human Experience

Space, Policy, and Society Research Group of the Massachusetts Institute of Technology

The Space, Policy, and Society Research Group of the Massachusetts Institute of Technology is an interdisciplinary collective of engineers, historians, and policy scholars working on subjects of national interest.

Despite common arguments that manned spaceflight brings advances of technology and the sciences, the true justification for the risk of human life and the spending of billions of dollars lies in the will of nations. Countries use their space programs as a means of proving technological capabilities and establishing or retaining their reputations as world powers. It is this purpose that will always drive space exploration and the innovations humanity dreams up to reach for the stars.

For such a highly technical endeavor, the rationales for human spaceflight have been surprisingly imprecise. What is the rationale for a large, government funded program of human space exploration? With the rapid growth in robotic and autonomous systems, does the equation for human versus remote exploration require rebalancing?

Nations have sent people into space for a variety of reasons in the past fifty years; some of them have become obso-

Space, Policy, and Society Research Group of the Massachusetts Institute of Technology, "The Future of Human Spaceflight," December 2008. Copyright © 2008 Massachusetts Institute of Technology. All rights reserved. Reproduced by permission.

lete in the face of changing technology, others remain salient for the future. The recent [President George W.] Bush vision gives a representative set: search for habitable worlds away from Earth, possibly leading to the discovery of present or past life on other planets; develop new technology; inspire children to study and seek careers in science, technology, engineering, and math; and symbolize American democracy to the world. Other rationales for humans in space include national security, scientific discovery, and establishing human colonies on other worlds.

Of course, each of these do partially justify human spaceflight. Human space flight has inspired, for example, many of today's scientists and engineers who witnessed the Apollo [lunar] program as children.

But science alone does not justify human missions to Mars.

Why Fly People into Space?

But which rationales apply uniquely to human spaceflight? What objectives might be achievable with remote spaceflight programs, or with other types of technology projects on the ground? For example, if the government wishes to support technology development, there are other, more direct ways to do so, such as R&D [research and development] contracts. Similarly, might the billions spent on space exploration be spent in other ways to support math and science education on the ground? (By comparison, the National Science Foundation's entire budget for education in math, science, and engineering was around $700 million in 2008, equivalent to just a few percent of NASA's [National Aeronautics and Space Administration] budget).

To structure the rationales for human spaceflight, we introduce the ideas of primary and secondary objectives. Primary objectives are those that can only be accomplished through the physical presence of human beings, those whose benefits exceed the opportunity costs, and those worthy of significant risk to, and possibly the loss of, human life. Primary objectives are exploration, national pride, and international prestige and leadership.

By contrast, secondary objectives have benefits that accrue from human presence in space but do not by themselves justify the cost or the risk. Secondary objectives include science, economic development and jobs, technology development, education, and inspiration.

Consider science in this frame-work. None doubt there are situations where people can accomplish things that machines cannot, or things that machines can only do more slowly than people and with greater difficulty. The flexible, dexterous manipulations of the human hand, for example, are still difficult to replicate with mechanisms. But few argue that the ability to drill into a planetary surface is sufficient justification for missions costing tens or hundreds of billions of dollars. Were human beings to walk on Mars they could of course accomplish significant science, potentially revolutionary discoveries, while there. But science alone does not justify human missions to Mars—the estimated cost would be many times the total budget of the National Science Foundation. Therefore science is a secondary objective of human spaceflight.

Similarly, if humans are to travel in space for long distances and durations, then it is ethically imperative to understand the biomedical implications of prolonged exposure to space and planetary environments. This entails understanding the biomedical impact of the microgravity environment of the ISS [International Space Station], the reduced gravity environments on the Moon (1/6g, or one-sixth the gravity of Earth), and on Mars (3/8g).

Understanding the influence of gravity on biological systems also has implications for health on Earth. But life science research does not stand by itself; it is necessary if we choose to send humans into space for other, primary reasons. Here on Earth, medical experimentation with humans is given serious ethical scrutiny and practical limitations, no matter how great the potential benefit. Human spaceflight purely for health research would likely be subject to similar ethical constraints. Thus human life science research is also a secondary objective of human spaceflight.

Economic and technology development have a similar status. First, there is the opportunity cost—if the U.S. government wishes to invest in technology, there are other more direct ways to fund it. Developing space-based life support technologies or moon-dust scrubber systems, for example, are not as likely to generate returns for earth-based applications as would direct investment in solar cell manufacturing or new biomaterials.

Another argument frames human spaceflight as a jobs program, employing tens of thousands of people on the ground. The Shuttle program, for example, employs over 2,000 civil servants and 15,000 work year equivalents for contractors. But again, few argue that human spaceflight is the only, or even the optimal way to invest in a technically talented workforce.

There are presently no known natural resources in space that can be profitably exploited. Even were such resources and an efficient extraction scheme to be discovered, it is unlikely that human presence would be required. Human presence will always be more expensive than remote operations, so any genuine space-based extractive business is likely to be heavily based on remote presence. Therefore technology and economic development are secondary objectives of human spaceflight.

None of this is to say that secondary objectives are unimportant; all have contributing roles to play in justifying government expenditures on space exploration. Secondary objectives may or may not justify their own costs, but in general they do not justify the risk to human life.

National Motives for Space Exploration

Human spaceflight is risky; seventeen people have died aboard U.S. spacecraft, and four aboard Russian craft. One in sixty Space Shuttle flights have ended in disaster. What objectives have sufficient value for nations and cultures that they justify these risks to life?

A primary objective of human spaceflight has been, and should be, exploration. Exploration, of course, is a keyword in the [George W.] Bush vision and in NASA's own terminology. Yet while the word is often used, it is rarely specified beyond lofty rhetoric and allusions to curiosity and frontiers. What is exploration, and why explore?

First, it is worth considering what exploration is not. Some argue that "exploration is in our DNA," that some fundamental, even genetic, human trait compels us as individuals and as nations to seek out new territory. The civilization that fails to expand geographically, the argument goes, will enter a state of permanent decline, always to be exceeded by other nations with more compelling wanderlust.

We reject these arguments about essential qualities of human nature. No historical evidence, no social science evidence, and no genetic evidence prove that human beings have an innate, universal compulsion to explore. In fact, space exploration is radically different from the kinds of geographical expansion that have marked human history because of its high degree of technical difficulty, the environments' extreme hostility to human life, and the total lack of encounters with other human cultures. Furthermore, if there were some grand universal compulsion to explore, we would find no compelling reason for the United States or any other nation to act now, as we would eventually migrate to the stars, regardless of our potentially fallible political decision making.

The exploration of space will continue if and only if governments or other large entities consider it within their interests and means to do so. Only a fraction of nations have ever found exploration valuable, and only a smaller fraction are now space faring.

Moreover, if exploration were simply a matter of finding out what lies beyond our immediate vicinity, then satisfying that curiosity would not require direct human presence. If we are primarily concerned with finding what's out there, then robotic spacecraft and other technologies can help us find out at a fraction of the cost and risk. In fact, many such machines are returning wondrous data every day. If an innate human curiosity is used as a justification for space exploration in general, it fails as a justification for human space exploration.

If exploration were simply a matter of finding out what lies beyond our immediate vicinity, then satisfying that curiosity would not require direct human presence.

Exploration is a human activity, undertaken by certain cultures at certain times for particular reasons. It has components of national interest, scientific research, and technical innovation, but is defined by none of them. We define exploration as an expansion of the realm of human experience, bringing people into new places, situations, and environments, expanding and redefining what it means to be human. What is the role of Earth in human life? Is human life fundamentally tied to the earth, or could it survive without the planet?

Human presence, and its attendant risk, turns a spaceflight into a story that is compelling to large numbers of people. Exploration also has a moral dimension because it is in effect a cultural conversation on the nature and meaning of human life. Exploration by this definition can only be accomplished by direct human presence and may be deemed worthy of the risk of human life.

As an example, the lasting impact of the Apollo program is not defined by specific technologies of interest to engineers nor even by scientific results known within a particular community. What made an impression on the people across the globe were images of human beings walking on another world. The feat stands as one of the notable moments in the twentieth century, the photograph of an Apollo 11 astronaut on the moon a global icon of modernity and peaceful technological achievement. Even today, interest in Apollo centers on the human experience. The twelve men who walked on the moon did something, experienced something, that no other people have done before or since. They expanded the realm of human experience.

The expansion of human experience might seem too universal to satisfy national interests, too general to appeal to practical policy considerations. Indeed the Apollo missions were undertaken "in peace for all mankind." Nevertheless, they were unmistakably branded as American, and that branding provided the major political impetus for the program. Apollo expanded what it meant to be human in uniquely American ways. Observers hailed American astronauts as paragons of self-reliance, individualism and other American virtues.

The twelve men who walked on the moon . . . expanded the realm of human experience.

Pride and Prestige on Display

Closely related to the exploration objective, then, are those of national pride and international prestige. Rockets and spacecraft are powerful symbols, and since its origins human spaceflight has been promoted and received as an indicator of national strength and purpose. During the Cold War, the Soviet Union and the United States upheld human spaceflight as the badge of national leadership, technological strength, and political resolve. Lyndon Johnson perhaps put it best when he said "In the eyes of the world first in space means first, period; second in space is second in everything." By this argument, any nation advanced and focused enough to send people into space must be set to define the future. Any nation that could muster the resources, master the technologies, and exhibit the long-term focus to mount human missions into space must be capable of other great feats, be they military, economic, or cultural.

By sending people into places and situations unprecedented in human history, nations aim to expand a global definition of humanity in their own image.

Though the Cold War rivalry has faded, its presumption that leadership in space correlated with economic, political, and cultural leadership had wide impact. As many observers have noted, human spaceflight is an instrument of soft power—it serves as an example for members of other nations and cultures to emulate and follow. Incorporating this logic as their own, other nations have accepted the notion that human spaceflight is a marker of modernity and first-class status. In China and Japan, not to mention numerous other nations who have flown people on American or Russian flights, astronauts remain public figures of iconic "rock star" status. When Russian President Vladimir Putin wrote to President Hu Jintao after the first Chinese human spaceflight, he congratulated him on the "successful advancement of your country along the path of comprehensive development, of its becoming a modern world power."

Nonetheless, all nations do not share the same rationales for human spaceflight. Each defines its own human space accomplishments according to its own cultural values. The Soviet Union, for example, hailed its cosmonauts as ideological icons of the communist regime, paragons of the "new Soviet man." As historian Slava Gerovitch writes, "the Soviet cosmonauts publicly represented a communist ideal, an active human agency of sociopolitical and economic change."

The Chinese similarly acclaim their taikonauts as embodiments of a Chinese history, culture, and technological prowess. As historian James Hansen has written, the cultural iconography surrounding China's first space traveler, Shenzhou V's Yang Liwei, evoked reactions mixing "pragmatic nationalism, communist ideology, traditional Confucian values, and [the] drive for economic and high-tech industrial competitiveness." In India, too, accomplishments in space represent national aspirations to become a global power.

By sending people into places and situations unprecedented in human history, nations aim to expand a global definition of humanity in their own image. The benefits to a country being represented in this way have generally justified the risk and cost of human life, much as military service to a nation is deemed worthy of such sacrifices.

Public perceptions of spaceflight vary unevenly among nations. For rising countries such as China and India, accomplishments in human spaceflight serve to announce their emergence into an elite club of global powers. Americans, more secure in recent decades of their nation's leadership in science and technology, seem to be less interested—few Americans can name a single active astronaut. American public perception could change quickly, however, in the face of foreign accomplishments (a Chinese landing on the moon, for example), or in light of a continued decline (real and perceived) in U.S. fortunes and status.

National pride and international prestige remain primary objectives of human spaceflight—achievable only with physical human presence and deemed by nations to be worth the financial cost and risk to human life.

Nevertheless, we recommend against reviving the Cold War model of the "space race," which will only serve to put

U.S. space policy in a reactive mode. Rather, the United States should take advantage of pride and prestige in human spaceflight to enhance its leadership and further cooperation rather than encourage competition.

9

Humans Should Plan to Colonize Space in Case of Global Catastrophe

Paul Johnson

Paul Johnson is an historian. His books include Modern Times, Intellectuals, A History of the American People, *and most recently,* Churchill.

Much of the worry over global warming is unwarranted because the theory lacks any consistency. Rather than concerning themselves with preventing a fictional disaster, scientists should focus on the more realistic goal of finding another planet on which to live in the event of a potential and real global catastrophe such as Earth's clash with a stray meteorite. Funding space colonization is no more expensive than throwing away money on climate change "solutions," and the endeavor would be much more productive to humankind as a whole.

The [2009] Copenhagen Summit [an international conference on climate change] was bound to fail if only because politicians are beginning to realize that ordinary voters do not believe in man-made Global Warming, as polls plainly show. They did not believe in Marxist Dialectical Materialism either, or Freudianism. These three pseudo-sciences have a lot in common, not least their ability to inspire a religious kind of belief in highly educated people who lack a genuine creed.

When I was an undergraduate the philosopher I studied most carefully was Karl Popper, especially his writings on the

Paul Johnson, "The Real Way to Save the Planet," *American Spectator*, vol. 43, no. 1, February 2010, pp. 40–41.

evaluation of evidence and criteria to distinguish a genuine scientific theory from a false one. He made two key points. First, a theory must include the falsifiability principle. It must be susceptible to empirical tests and, if it fails to meet them, be scrapped. He gave as an example of a genuine theory [Albert] Einstein's General Relativity of 1915. Einstein insisted that it must survive three practical tests, and if it failed any one of them be dropped as untrue. In fact it passed triumphantly all three, beginning in 1919, and many other since.

Popper argued that prima facie [at first sight] evidence of a bogus theory was the practice of altering or enlarging it, by its authors, to accommodate new evidence since its original formulation. This, he argued, had happened in the case of Marxism and, still more, Freudianism. Scientific theories, he argued, must be very precise and scientific to be of any use. Marxism and Freudianism were just portmanteau [combining many qualities] notions into which virtually any kind of phenomena could be made to fit. Hence Marxism led to political and economic disaster areas like the Soviet Union, and Freudianism to a stupendous waste of time and money.

Global Warming Is a Myth

It is a pity Popper did not live to see that Global Warming fit perfectly into his model of a pseudo-theory. It is vaguely and imprecisely formulated. It fails the falsifiability test, because all new evidence is made to fit by enlarging the theory. When originally formulated in the 1980s, Global Warming produced by man-made emissions would lead, it was argued, to much higher temperatures and desiccation. There would be a huge drop in rainfall and an imperative need to build seawater desalination plants. I recall an unusually dry summer (1987) in the English Lake District, normally rainy, was triumphantly presented as "absolute proof" of the theory. This autumn, the Lake District had an unusually wet spell, culminating in floods that engulfed the delightful town of Cockermouth, where [poet William] Wordsworth was born. This was pounced upon by Global Warming "experts" as "absolute proof" of their theory, and paraded as such in Copenhagen.

The fact is that the theory has now been expanded to include any unusual form of weather, anywhere. Hot summers, warm winters—global warming. Cold weather at an unusual time of year—global warming. Drought, storms, floods—global warming. No snow on the ski slopes, sudden snow, out of season snow, very heavy snow—global warming. Of course in countries like Japan or the UK [United Kingdom], where unusual, unpredictable, and tiresomely variable weather is the norm (it was first commented on in the UK by the Venerable Bede [an English monk and scholar] in the eighth century), the public does not swallow global warming, and polls show majorities of 55 to 60 percent reject it.

Of course vested interests accept it. It is regarded as a splendid way of damaging the American economy, by the same kind of left-wing intellectuals who supported the Club of Rome [a global think tank] in the 1960s, which argued that world resources were on the brink of exhaustion. It is a form of pantheism and a useful emotional outlet for people who have renounced Judeo-Christianity. If someone is anti-American, left-liberal, and atheist, it is virtually certain he (or even she: women are notoriously more skeptical about it than men are) is a Global Warmer.

Vast sums of money will continue to be spent on an unproven and unprovable theory, predicting a global catastrophe from the realms of fantasy.

Then again, global warming now has a powerful, worldwide institutional substructure. If a media outlet has an environment correspondent, or a university a Department of Climate Studies, or a government a Ministry of Global Warming, those involved are certain to be not just believers but fanatical propagandists for the cause. Their livelihood depends on it. I calculate that the lobby now includes over 20,000 full-time, well-paid professionals whose entire life is spent in pushing "proofs." The existence of this enormous phalanx of well-placed, articulate enthusiasts has inevitably led to the capture of powerful institutions—in Britain, for instance, the Meteorological Office, the Royal Society, and the BBC, together with many universities and newspapers. It used to be supposed that scientists, or those calling themselves such, were incorruptible and guided purely by genuine convictions based on objective evidence. But scientists behave just like politicians if the pressure and prizes make it worth their while to conform.

Scientists Must Shift Priorities

So vast sums of money will continue to be spent on an unproven and unprovable theory, predicting a global catastrophe from the realms of fantasy. The money could be much more profitably spent on space exploration. This is a genuine science and could turn out to be useful, even vital. The planet Earth, though not threatened with destruction by man-made global warming, is by no means indestructible. There are many unpredictable events within our solar system, and still more outside it, that could make Earth uninhabitable by humans. A meteorite of sufficient size could destroy it entirely. A giant sunspot could produce precisely the catastrophic climate change the lobby falsely claims is being created by man's "emissions." There are hundreds of fatal possibilities astrophysicists can imagine, and thousands more, no doubt, that could occur.

In the long term, it is desirable that the human race, faced with the prospect of extinction on Earth, should prepare an escape route for itself to another inhabitable planet. In order to do this we must explore the universe far more thoroughly and exhaustively than we have done up till now, and equally important, develop the concept of mass space travel and colonization schemes. Mankind has done this before, notably in the 15th century, when the threat of plague and starvation in Europe led to the successful crossing of the Atlantic and colonization in the Americas. We need to repeat the imaginative effort of the late medieval Spanish, Portuguese, and Genoans in navigation, technology, and courage, but on an infinitely greater scale. This would be a worthy cause for the united resources of the human race to combine in furthering—the colonization of the universe.

It may be a distant goal, but it is a practical one, and in pursuing it we would do more to unite the human race in purposeful activity than anything else so far proposed. By contrast, combating a largely imaginary threat of global warming is just as costly, as well as scientifically unsound, technologically impossible, and, not least, divisive.

10

Space Colonization Is Impractical

Peter N. Spotts

Peter N. Spotts is a staff writer at the Christian Science Monitor.

Although some foresee humans building installations and settlements in space and on the moon or another planet, the reality check provided by the spacewalk repairs in November of 2007 shows this to be a dream. The dream overlooks operational problems and maintenance. The spacewalk repairs required a small army of engineers and astronauts from three countries in order to be carried out successfully. The farther away from planet Earth that you get, the more difficult and costly it is to design fixable equipment and handle equipment failure.

Saturday's spacewalk [in November 2007] to fix a ripped solar panel on the International Space Station [ISS] might be likened to threading cords through grommets of a camping tarp—except that the "tarp" was gently waving and electrically charged and the "repairman" was standing on the top rung of a stepladder attached to another stepladder.

The repair means the panels will be able to provide electricity for the space station. But it also points to the vital role that on-orbit maintenance will play—and the exacting demands it imposes—as visionaries set their sights on outposts and factories on the moon or Mars or on hotels and commercial laboratories orbiting high above Earth.

For engineers, the long-term challenge is to design simpler, more forgiving hardware for use in space. But for those dreaming of living on and beyond low-Earth orbit, Saturday's spacewalk is a reality check about what it takes to keep deep-space facilities running—and about the risks to people and investments if repairs fail.

The farther from Earth astronauts travel, the more acute maintenance challenges become.

Wake Up Call

The solar-panel spacewalk was "really kind of a wake-up call," says Adam Bruckner, who heads the aeronautics and astronautics department in the University of Washington's College of Engineering. Concepts for colonizing the moon or for commercial facilities on orbit "are interesting," he says, "but when you actually . . . think about doing it over there, a lot of the maintenance . . . and operational problems have been swept under the rug."

As reality TV, "Survivor" has nothing on Saturday's webcast of the tense, seven-hour spacewalk by astronauts Scott Parazynski and Col. Douglas Wheelock. Earlier in the week, the shuttle and station crews had moved a solar-panel assembly from a temporary spot on the ISS to its permanent location at one end of the station's backbone, or truss. As the space-station crew tried to unfurl the panels on Oct. 30, segments of one of the assembly's four wing-like arrays snagged and ripped, halting the deployment.

From engineers on the ground devising a repair strategy to Dr. Parazynski himself, the repair effort stretched everyone and everything to their limits, notes Derek Hassmann, the lead flight director for the shuttle mission.

Parazynski made the repairs farther from the airlock than any astronaut had ever been, his boots locked onto an extension at the end of a 50-foot boom. The station's robotic arm, in turn, gripped the boom like a relay runner's baton. (Picture those stepladders stacked one atop another.) Colonel Wheelock, meanwhile, tethered himself to the truss at the base of the solar array to serve as spotter for Parazynski and the crew members operating the robotic arm.

Once near the panel, the 6-foot, 2-inch Parazynski stretched to his physical limit in order to thread cuff-link-like cords through grommets in the array, which held it together when he cut the frayed wire that had snagged the segments. Each step required subtle moves by the boom operators. Parazynski had to remain close enough to the array to do the work. But he also had to keep far enough away to avoid the risk of electrical shock from the "live" solar cells or further damage to the array as the boom and array shifted back and forth in response to his movements. The boom-robotic arm combo stretched to within two inches of its maximum reach.

Encountering Problems

Typically, astronauts spend weeks, even months, training for an assembly spacewalk that makes no use of robotic arms, says Mr. Hassmann. For Saturday's spacewalk, a small army of engineers and astronauts in the US, Canada, and Russia worked around the clock to devise the repair strategy and to make or modify the tools needed to pull off the repair.

"People always said that we're going to encounter problems we can't even think of right now and have to be ready for them in some way," says Tom Jones, a former shuttle astronaut who conducted spacewalks to help attach the US lab module Destiny to the space station in 2001. "Well, here it is, that actual unexpected. And it always throws everybody a curve. We'd better get used to this."

The farther from Earth astronauts travel, the more acute maintenance challenges become, notes Larry Bell of the Sasakawa International Center for Space Architecture at the University of Houston.

Planners try to build redundancy into critical systems and to provide the tools and materials for making some repairs. Indeed, one tool Parazynski used to handle the undulating solar array took shape from a sheet of Teflon and some insulating tape in the space station's workshop. But mission planners always face a trade-off between trying to plan for maintenance needs and keeping materials within the weight limits during launch.

Especially when talking about trips to the moon or Mars, "it's a long way back to the hardware store," Dr. Bell says.

What comes through loud and clear is that just as the 30-year-old space shuttle remains an experimental craft, the space station as well as habitats on the moon and Mars are, and will be, experimental in their own ways.

Coping in Space

For the people involved in such repairs, coping requires several things, specialists say. Managers must make quick decisions about which problems are most crucial to fix, for instance. Crew members must be sufficiently trained and practiced in generic mechanical and spacewalking skills to allow them quickly to adapt what they've learned to unforeseen problems.

As for hardware, Russia's experience with the Mir space station may hold some lessons, Dr. Jones suggests. Its space-station segments essentially were plug-and-play; no spacewalks were needed to make the newly attached modules habitable. But that meant snaking power and cooling lines inside the hull, something ISS designers tried to avoid for safety reasons as well as for more flexibility in configuring the station's various elements. Still, it will be important to reduce the number of adjustments or amount of handwork newly arriving crew members must perform, Jones says.

What comes through loud and clear is that just as the 30-year-old space shuttle remains an experimental craft, the space station as well as habitats on the moon and Mars are, and will be, experimental in their own ways.

"In space, there's no such thing as run-of-the-mill," Dr. Bruckner observes.

11

Faster-Than-Light Travel Is Worth Pursuing

Hal Plotkin

Hal Plotkin is the Silicon Valley correspondent for CNBC.com, *technology columnist for* SFGate.com, *and a member of the Foothill–De Anza Community College District Governing Board of Trustees.*

While current scientific knowledge claims that faster-than-light travel is impossible, humankind should not give up in pursuing this dream. Scientists should begin thinking outside of traditional conceptions of physics and re-evaluate modes of thinking. Too much of modern physics is based on the way matter behaves on Earth; perhaps bringing experiments into outer space will lead to a breakthrough. Pushed along by new models from theoretical physics, the advent of faster-than-light travel may still be in the offing.

In the two years I've been at this column [for *SFGate.com*], I've been overwhelmed by the many intelligent and well-informed e-mails that have come pouring in.

The response has been so good I've decided to go out on a bit of a limb.

An idea has been kicking around in the back of my head for nearly 20 years now and I've long wondered what, if any, merit it might have.

I figure one or more of my readers might know.

It concerns what may be the most important technical question of all time:

Will we ever be able to travel faster than the speed of light?

Like it or not, our current understanding of physics tells us we humans are pretty much stuck in this solar system.

An Impossibility According to Modern Physics

The answer is critically important because if nature really does have a cosmic speed limit, it means all those "*Star Trek* fantasies" about interstellar travel will forever be just that, fantasies. Even the closest large clusters of stars visible in the night sky are thousands of light years distant.

Like it or not, our current understanding of physics tells us we humans are pretty much stuck in this solar system. That is, until our sun eventually uses up all its stored energy in about 5 billion years or so and collapses, taking along with it any nearby life that might still be around.

Faster-than-light travel may be the only technology that could save humanity from extinction.

But if [Albert] Einstein was right, faster-than-light travel will never happen.

Einsteinian physics tells us that anyone traveling that fast will be crushed into a tiny sliver of their former selves because mass increases with velocity.

The faster any type of matter moves, the denser it's thought to become.

That's why most scientists agree that physical travel at or even near light speed is simply impossible.

But science has been wrong before. A little over 50 years ago, for example, conventional engineering wisdom held that controlled flight past the speed of sound was physically impossible. Back then more than a few respected thinkers agreed that sonic shock waves would cause airplanes to lose control or to break up into tiny pieces. Those fears gained credence when the first few pilots who attempted supersonic travel died trying.

But in 1947, the team behind famed aviator Chuck Yeager finally figured out how to take the necessary precautions that led to the first successful hypersonic flight. Not only was it possible, Yeager later wrote, but the ride was so smooth "Grandma could be up there sipping lemonade."

It's unlikely Grandma will be sipping lemonade while traveling at light-speed anytime soon. The physical obstacles to faster-than-light travel appear insurmountable, especially when compared with something as simple as overcoming the effects of vibrations caused by a sonic boom.

Experimenting in Outer Space

Even so, I've been thinking about what strikes me as a simple and intuitive way to further test whether it will ever be possible to get anyone or anything moving that fast.

It would involve an experiment conducted in outer space, where factors such as gravity and friction caused by the atmosphere wouldn't complicate things.

Here's the idea:

First, imagine a thin rod one mile long in outer space, situated somewhere between Earth and a neighboring planet. Then imagine a motor at the exact center of the rod, at the half-mile point, that spins the rod such that the center of the rod rotates once per second. (Think of a long, thin baton being twirled in space. Each end of the baton makes one full circle with each single rotation.)

If you remember your high school geometry, the circumference of a circle is calculated by multiplying its diameter by Pi.

So, assuming the one-mile-long baton maintains its structural integrity, each of its ends will travel Pi, or roughly 3.141592654 miles in the one second it took for one rotation.

For the sake of simplicity, let's say each end of the rod travels 3 miles per second, just to make the next calculation easier.

Now, the speed of light in a vacuum is about 186,000 miles per second. That means if we can stretch the rod to one-third that length, or 62,000 miles long, and get it spinning in space once per second, the ends of the rod would have to be moving faster than the speed of light.

Which, at least according to theory, would be totally impossible.

And, to be sure, building a 62,000-mile rod in space and getting it spinning once per second would be an unimaginably cumbersome task.

Fortunately, however, we already have motors here on Earth capable of spinning things hundreds, even thousands of times faster than that. The disk drive in my computer, for example.

The quicker we can spin the baton in space, the shorter it needs to be for the ends of the baton to approach super-fast velocities. Even better, the ends of the baton would reach those speeds while the baton itself stays in the same physical location in space where it can easily be observed.

So, it might be possible to use centrifugal motion of the sort described above to push matter we can observe in nearby space to approach or—in the unlikely event Einstein missed something—maybe even exceed the speed of light using a baton or rod that's just a few miles long, perhaps far shorter.

And, imagine that it's not a rod or a baton at all. Imagine it's just a stiff iron thread; all of a sudden a totally impractical experiment becomes far more manageable.

Iron might be a good material to use since it's the super-dense matter nature leaves behind when giant stars have consumed their energy. But a non-conducting material might be a better choice. Figuring out which materials work best, even if none work perfectly, would be an added benefit.

For the record, one of the main arguments against even attempting such a thing goes something like this: We already know how matter reacts when it approaches the speed of light because we've seen what happens when we get some individual particles moving at those speeds in particle accelerators such as those at Lawrence Berkeley Laboratory and the Centre Europeen de Recherche Nucleaire, or CERN, in Geneva.

The predicted result sees the bar bending in space well before it reaches the speed of light until no amount of force can get it to move any faster.

Since all matter is made up of particles, the theory goes, we already know how larger pieces of matter will behave because we know what happens to their parts.

But that argument has always troubled me.

Are Current Scientists Thinking Too Narrowly?

At best, earthbound particle accelerators tell us how individual particles act when subjected to certain conditions. But they can't and don't tell us much about how groups of particles, or other even smaller as yet undetected particles, might interact with each other when closely bound under the most extreme conditions.

It's kind of like trying to figure out what's happening on the freeway by looking at just one car. Or, to stretch another analogy, it's similar to the way modern medicine sometimes treats one symptom without realizing it's really part of some larger problem.

I have no specific evidence that physics suffers from a similar too-narrow focus. But it seems to be at least a possibility.

There are, of course, compelling reasons to believe Einstein had it right all along. There have, after all, been numerous experimental observations that have supported his many conclusions.

But we've never actually seen what happens when large quantities of matter approach the speed of light. That may be because it is in fact impossible. Or it may be because we just haven't figured out how to do it yet.

That's because so far it's been impossible to test on earth, in part because anything moving that fast in any one direction would quickly race away from us before we could see what happened to it.

At best, earthbound particle accelerators tell us how individual particles act when subjected to certain conditions.

What's more, the twirling baton experiment also would not work here on Earth because friction caused by the atmosphere would incinerate anything moving that fast.

Pre-Space Age scientists responded to those obstacles by envisioning the large particle accelerators we now have that use magnets and vacuum conditions to send tiny particles of matter hurtling at velocities that come within a whisker of light speed. The particles are then smashed into one another, or into other substances, in hopes of breaking them apart to see what smaller particles might lie within.

We've been looking at the trees. But given the opportunities that space-based light speed experiments afford, we might learn even more by taking another look at the forest.

The hunt for a better understanding of these issues becomes even more exciting when you realize that modern physics requires almost, but not quite, as many leaps of faith as does modern religion.

It Is Too Early for a Definitive Answer

A consensus is now apparently emerging, for example, that all matter might be made up of invisibly tiny vibrating loops of a stringlike substance. Put unforgivably simply, the theory is that the frequencies of each loop's vibrations are what determine the more familiar properties of matter that can be observed.

But what is the most fundamental building block of matter?

The truth is no one knows for sure because we haven't seen it yet.

Given that, one wonders if there might be a little arrogance reflected in the assumption that science already knows how all matter behaves under all possible conditions.

Although they're still very much in the minority, several theorists have recently suggested there could be a related way to create distortions in space that might allow faster-than-light travel.

We've been looking at the trees. But given the opportunities that space-based light speed experiments afford, we might learn more by taking another look at the forest.

Most mainstream physicists scoff at such possibilities. But some of the best of them, such as U.C. [University of California] Riverside's Philip Gibbs leave open at least the possibility that new knowledge may yet emerge.

Even if faster-than-light travel isn't possible, we could still learn a lot about materials sciences and other related topics by taking the problem back from the theorists who now own it. Trial and error approaches almost always yield far better science than is achieved by a reliance on conventional wisdom or untested assumptions.

Who knows, even if it didn't pass warp speed we might still end up with something like an interstellar catapult that could conceivably prove useful in other ways.

Spinning a thread in space might not let us travel faster than light. But I wonder if it might help us test our limits.

12

Faster-Than-Light Travel Is Impossible

Ian O'Neill

Ian O'Neill, who holds a doctorate in solar physics, is a space science producer at Discovery News and he also runs a science-based website.

Quantum physics makes it impossible for mankind to achieve faster-than-light travel. Not only is there no technology in existence to power a ship beyond light speed, even with a hypothetical generator capable of faster-than-light travel, the radiation produced as a byproduct would kill anyone onboard the vessel. This essentially eliminates any possibility of manned travel at speeds faster than the speed of light.

Just when I was getting excited about the possibility of travelling to distant worlds, scientists have uncovered a deep flaw with faster-than-light-speed travel. There appears to be a quantum limit on how fast an object can travel through space-time, regardless of whether we are able to create a bubble in space-time or not ...

First off, we have no clue about how to generate enough energy to create a "bubble" in space-time. This idea was first put on a scientific grounding [by] Michael Alcubierre from the University of Mexico in 1994, but before that was only popularized by science fiction universes such as *Star Trek*. However, to create this bubble we need some form of *exotic* matter fuel some *hypothetical* energy generator to output 10^{45} Joules (according to calculations by Richard K. Obousy and Gerald Cleaver in the paper "Putting the Warp into Warp Drive"). Physicists are not afraid of big numbers, and we are not afraid of words like "hypothetical" and "exotic", but to put this energy in perspective, we would need to turn all of Jupiter's mass into energy to even hope to distort space-time around an object.

This is a lot of energy.

If a sufficiently advanced human race *could* generate this much energy, I would argue that we would be masters of our Universe anyway, who would need warp drive when we could just as well create wormholes, star gates or access parallel universes. Yes, warp drive is science fiction, but it's interesting to investigate this possibility and open up physical scenarios where warp drive might work. Let's face it, anything less than light-speed travel is a real downer for our potential to travel to other star systems, so we need to keep our options open, no matter how futuristic.

Although warp speed is highly theoretical, at least it is based on some real physics. It's a mix of superstring and multi-dimensional theory, but warp speed seems to be possible, assuming a vast supply of energy. If we can "simply" squash the tightly curled extra-dimensions (greater than the "normal" four we live in) in front of a futuristic spacecraft and expand them behind, a bubble of stationary space will be created for the spacecraft to reside in. This way, the spaceship isn't travelling faster than light inside the bubble, the bubble itself is zipping through the fabric of space-time, facilitating faster-than-light-speed travel. *Easy.*

Not so fast.

Faster-Than-Light Travel Is Dangerous

According to new research on the subject, quantum physics has something to say about our dreams of zipping through space-time faster than c [the speed of light]. What's more, Hawking radiation would most likely cook anything inside this theoretical space-time bubble anyway. The Universe does not want us to travel faster than the speed of light.

"On one side, an observer located at the center of a super-luminal warp-drive bubble would generically experience a thermal flux of Hawking particles," says Stefano Finazzi and co-authors from the International School for Advanced Studies in Trieste, Italy. "On the other side, such Hawking flux will be generically extremely high if the exotic matter supporting the warp drive has its origin in a quantum field satisfying some form of Quantum Inequalities."

In short, Hawking radiation (usually associated with the radiation of energy and therefore loss of mass of evaporating black holes) will be generated, irradiating the occupants of the bubble to unimaginably high temperatures. The Hawking radiation will be generated as horizons will form at the front and rear of the bubble. Remember those big numbers physicists aren't afraid of? Hawking radiation is predicted to roast anything inside the bubble to a possible 10^{30}K (the *maximum possible* temperature, the Planck temperature, is 10^{32}K).

The Universe does not want us to travel faster than the speed of light.

Even if we could overcome this obstacle, Hawking radiation appears to be symptomatic of an even bigger problem; the space-time bubble would be unstable, on a quantum level.

"Most of all, we find that the RSET [renormalized stress-energy tensor] will exponentially grow in time close to, and on, the front wall of the superluminal bubble. Consequently, one is led to conclude that the warp-drive geometries are unstable against semiclassical back-reaction," Finazzi adds.

However, if you wanted to create a space-time bubble for subluminal (less-than light speed) travel, no horizons form, and therefore no Hawking radiation is generated. In this case, you might not be beating the speed of light, but you do have a fast, and stable way of getting around the Universe. Unfortunately we still need "exotic" matter to create the space-time bubble in the first place . . .

13

Humans Eventually Will Encounter Alien Life

Frank Drake, interviewed by Wilson da Silva

Frank Drake is an astronomer and astrophysicist who is noted for deriving the Drake Equation, a formula used to estimate the number of extraterrestrial civilizations in the Milky Way. He also is the founder of Search for Extraterrestrial Intelligence (SETI), collaborative projects working toward contact with alien life forms. Wilson da Silva is the co-founder and editor-in-chief of Cosmos *magazine.*

Though fifty years have passed since the founding of SETI, many of the signals sent into space have touched only a fraction of the stars known to be in the Milky Way. There still is much more space to search. Eventually, though, humans will make contact with another intelligent form of life. The public remains interested in alien contact, and the science is improving; the only obstacle to overcome is time.

Less than a month before turning 30, Frank Drake flipped a switch and started listening to the stars. It was 8 April 1960, and Project Ozma—the first ever SETI [Search for Extraterrestrial Intelligence] search—had begun.

And although 50 years have passed with no clear evidence of extraterrestrials out there, Drake remains convinced that humanity has barely scratched the surface. The search has barely begun.

His influence in the search for extraterrestrial intelligence—or SETI, as it is commonly known—has been enormous.

Drake not only conducted the first radio search for civilisations beyond Earth, he helped Carl Sagan design [the] plaque in 1972 that was attached to the Pioneer 10 and 11 spacecraft, the first of humanity's emissaries to leave the Solar System.

The search [for extraterrestrial life] has barely begun.

In 1974, to mark the reopening of the Arecibo radio dish in Puerto Rico—the world's largest—he transmitted humanity's first interstellar message: a three-minute binary signal with a pictogram of DNA, a graphic of the Solar System, and 10 other items meant to describe our world to extraterrestrials. It was aimed at the globular star cluster M13 some 25,000 light years away.

But he is best known for creating the enormously influential equation that bears his name—the Drake Equation.

Devised in 1961 ... it seeks to quantify the unquantifiable: the potential number of extraterrestrial civilisations in our galaxy. And it is still used today.

The following is an interview conducted with the SETI pioneer in February 2010.

[Silva:] *When you talk about your famous equations, what do you think all the years after you first published it?*

[Drake:] People keep asking, 'should the equation be changed?' The answer is no. It still works. It's still correct.

The only thing that's changed is the numbers we put into it. When I first invented the equation we had to guess some of the factors in the equation. A lot of those have now been established through observation. For instance the fraction of stars that have planets—we know now that it is more than half. The number of possible habitable planets in a system is higher than we thought in the past—because we've discovered things such as oceans in places we thought they couldn't exist, such as Europa.

So the equation is still good. The numbers we put in it are getting more accurate all the time. There are still some big unknowns. One is the fraction of civilisations that actually develop technology. The other is—the big factor is—the longevity, the *I-factor*, which we will not know until we've discovered some other civilisations.

Have you been surprised by some of the developments? For example, the number of exoplanets out there?

Oh yeah. Well, surprised in a good way. We used to make estimates based on very indirect observations of the rotations of planets, and theoretical models. Well, now we have actual observation confirmation that those things were correct.

The observations have all supported the idea that there is a lot of life in the universe. What they show is that what happened in the Solar System was not unusual. It did not require any special circumstances, or any freak situations, and therefore what happened here should have happened in many places, and that includes the evolution of an intelligent technology-using creature.

What would you think would be the impact on humanity if we finally find aliens out there?

It will have a tremendous impact because almost any civilisation we find will be much older than our own. They will have much more experience. Much more knowledge, technical and scientific. And that will benefit us greatly. And we will learn ways to have a higher quality of life on earth which would otherwise take us perhaps hundreds of years of expensive research to learn, to identify ourselves.

It's been 50 years since Project Ozma. You were quite excited in the early years when you began. Has your point-of-view changed? Or your impressions changed about the likelihood of finding intelligent civilisations?

No. I've always known it was very improbable. If you put the most optimistic figures in the Drake Equation, it leads you to conclude that probably only one in ten million stars has a detectable signal. We haven't nearly searched that many stars.

There's also the problem of we don't know what frequency to look at. We're presently still limited to not searching all reasonable frequencies.

What happened here should have happened in many places, and that includes the evolution of an intelligent technology-using creature.

Also the signals may be transient, they may not be 'on' all the time, so we need to search tens of millions of stars for long periods of time on a wide band of frequencies, before we'll have a good chance of succeeding. And we haven't done that.

So, if anything, you now appreciate how much harder the problem is?

We knew it was hard in the beginning, now it's clear that we were right. It is hard.

Now that 50 years have gone by, is your overall attitude still one of optimism? Or is it optimism weighed down with some frustration?

Well, it's optimism with reality that it's going to take a long, long time to succeed. But we will succeed.

Can you venture a time frame?

That is very difficult to do. It depends on how many resources we put into it. Which depends on the will of governments, and funding sources. Which has been changing greatly from year to year.

I'm guessing twenty to thirty years. *Guess.* 'Guess' is the right word.

In the general public and in popular culture, the enthusiasm for space and alien life has somewhat declined. Do you think that this might impair the search?

Well, if the interest declines, that's bad. But I don't think it has declined. There's a tremendous interest in science-fiction movies. The most popular movies of all time, except for *Titanic*, were all science-fiction movies. There's a tremendous interest in the general public in life in space.

But the general public also realises that finding life is going to be difficult, and that in a way we [SETI researchers] have hurt ourselves, by raising false expectations.

The chances of success are small.

NASA [National Aeronautics and Space Administration] does that too. They say that every mission they send is going to determine whether there is life on some place, and no mission they've ever sent could, could find that out. And the public begins to become cynical about claims of 'Oh, something's gonna detect life in space. Well, we've heard that before, and it was not true.'

It's a problem we have: the media glorifies something, glorifies our search more than it deserves. Our search is very limited. The chances of success are small. Often the media don't make that clear.

When we say '50 years', it's really, if you tally it all up, only thousands of hours. Isn't it?

Well, it's more than that. Actually, it's a lot more than that, because of these searches that are continuing watching, such as SETI@Home, conducted by Harvard University.

The researchers there just let the Earth rotate, and they can say, 'well, we looked at thousands of stars'. In fact, they look at any given star for 10 seconds, and they look down a very narrow band of frequencies, so it's very misleading.

You say you've looked at a thousand stars, but you've looked at each one for a few seconds at a few frequencies. Well . . . that hardly counts.

In some searches, such as Project Phoenix, they did look for a long time at stars, and a wide band of frequencies, and that was a much more thorough search. The amount of searching we've done is highly variable in its quality. A lot of it is almost worthless.

That's because we don't know what will succeed, therefore we're trying so many different strategies.

Ah, that's right. And also many of the searches have been very weak in that they have no immediate follow-up. For instance, in the Harvard Search, in SETI@Home, the data is recorded, is not analysed for typically at least days, or usually weeks, later. And they will find something that looks like a signal.

Then they go back and look at that place in the sky and that frequency and there's nothing there. That tells you nothing. It could be that these signals are present only for 10 minutes every month or so, and so the fact that there isn't an immediate follow-up is very damaging. It greatly reduces your chances of success.

The only search that's been able to follow-up immediately is our search [run by the SETI Institute]. And that's because we have enough money to have people present. And it's a matter of money.

That's important, isn't it? Being able to follow-up?

It's no good detecting a signal if you can't identify it immediately. And it needs to be immediately, because the signal may be transient. It may be briefly there. And there are a lot of scenarios you can concoct which would have all the signals being transient. In our searches—we *can* follow-up—none of the candidates has proved to be extraterrestrial. Some searches have hundreds of unexplained signals that we'll never know what they are.

Of the different strategies that have been used or suggested— radio signals, optical signals, etc.—is there one that you are sort of most confident about?

That's a hard one.

Optical is much more detectable, because of these very powerful lasers. However, there's a big down side to that, as they are much more detectable *if* the light pulse is focussed by a very large reflector, which means that the amount of space that sees that pulse is very, very small. In fact, they have to be intentionally aiming it at you.

Some searches have hundreds of unexplained signals that we'll never know what they are.

So, the optical only works if other civilisations are intentionally trying to signal. Which would mean they know about our system, and where our planets are. That raises a whole new issue, which is whether there is altruism in the universe.

What do you suspect is the detectable number of civilisations in the galaxy now, knowing what we know now about exoplanets and so forth?

Ten thousand. That number is largely based on a guess as to the longevity being about ten thousand years. It's totally a guess, because it's far beyond our experience.

But that's now? Detectable now?

Right now.

14

Humans Are Unlikely Ever to Encounter Alien Life

Iain Murray

Iain Murray is former associate editor of The American Enterprise, *a former news organ of the American Enterprise Institute, a conservative, public policy research organization.*

One of the ultimate goals of space exploration has always been to discover and make contact with other intelligent life. Despite scientists' constant attempts, no contact has been made, nor has anyone discovered hints of other life forms in the vastness of space. While mathematicians claim discovery of life elsewhere to be inevitable, the evidence points to the liklihood that mankind is alone in the universe.

As a long-time devotee of science fiction, I have always been excited by the possibility that mankind might encounter extraterrestrial life. But I have always tried to apply the rules of logic and reason to those prospects. And it is becoming increasingly clear to me, and others, that merely wanting to believe is not enough.

As our observation methods have improved, we've learned that somewhere on the order of 20–50 percent of all stars have planets orbiting them. We have no idea whether life-friendly planets are common, or what the chances are that life, much less intelligent life, exists on such planets, but if we assume that there is nothing special about our own solar system, we come up with some pretty optimistic numbers. Astronomers Frank Drake and Carl Sagan suggested that there could be 10 million civilizations as advanced as or more advanced than us in the galaxy today.

Such a theory, however, begs an important question, one raised by Italian physicist Enrico Fermi way back in 1950. He turned to his lunch partners at Los Alamos [National Laboratory], who included [American physicist] Edward Teller, and asked simply, "Where is everybody?" If intelligent, communicating life is common, why haven't we seen evidence of it? After all, if the formation of civilizations has been fairly constant through the long life of the universe, then there should have been billions of them by now.

Even if every single other civilization that has existed over the vast life of our galaxy had chosen not to send out probes, we should still be able to pick up their traces.

While the galaxy is a big place, it's also been around for a very long time, more than long enough for intelligent life to have placed signs throughout the galaxy. Los Alamos physicist John von Neumann calculated that self-replicating probes traveling at one fortieth the speed of light could spread through the entire galaxy in just 4 million years. That may sound like a long time, but the universe is more than three thousand times older than that, so there has been ample time for intelligent life to show itself if it exists outside our miraculous planet.

Even if every single other civilization that has existed over the vast life of our galaxy had chosen not to send out probes, we should still be able to pick up their traces. Most physicists who have studied the issue agree that if civilizations want to be heard, then we have the capacity to detect their most likely means of sending out signals.

Science Has Found No Intelligent Life

But in 40 years of searching, we have detected no such signal. In 1967, we thought we had one, but that turned out to be the entirely natural signal of a pulsar. Ten years later, the Ohio State University Big Ear observatory detected a 37-second burst of activity that prompted astronomer Jerry Ehman to write, "Wow!" in the signal's margin. Yet attempts to find the Wow signal again have been unsuccessful; it seems likely now that it came from the mundane source of a manmade earth satellite. Yet the skies are vast, and there's a lot of material out there. So radio observatories are using the dispersed computer power of millions of interested PC owners who have agreed to let software run on their computers during down times to search for artificial signals. In six years, all those millions of computers have come up with just one candidate, a signal named SHGb02+ 14a, with a frequency of 1420 megahertz, which has important ties to the element hydrogen. This makes it a good candidate for being artificial, because signals tied to the laws of physics or mathematics are much more likely to be understood by an alien civilization than anything else. Even so, the SETI [Search for Extraterrestrial Intelligence] astronomers are not optimistic. It comes from a point in space with no star system within 1,000 light years. "We're not jumping up and down, but we are continuing to observe it," says Dan Werthimer, a University of California radio astronomer.

We are therefore led to the uncomfortable conclusion that there may be something wrong with the assumption that life can exist in numerous other places. Perhaps our solar system is not average at all. Perhaps life-friendly planets are rare. That is the conclusion of University of Washington scientists Peter Ward and David Brownlee, whose book, *Rare Earth*, caused a sensation when first published in 2000.

Ward and Brownlee point out that not all areas of the universe are hospitable to life. Our sun is "a star rich in metal, a star found in a safe region of a spiral galaxy, a star moving very slowly on its galactic pinwheel . . . not near an active gamma ray source, not in a multiple star system, not even in a binary, or near a pulsar, or near stars too small, too large, or soon to go supernova." That's quite a lengthy list of useful coincidences. And the theory goes on.

Chances of Finding Life Are Slim

Earth, it appears, is fortunate in being placed right in the middle of a "habitable zone" around our star. We are one Astronomic Unit (AU) from the sun. Michael Hart and others have worked out the habitable zone as being between 0.95 AU and 1.15 AU. Only about 10 percent of stars with planets are likely to have a planet in a habitable zone.

Moreover, all the planets we've so far discovered around other stars are gas giants, like Jupiter. Most of them orbit much closer to their suns than Jupiter does, or have eccentric orbits. If either of these had happened in our solar system, any Earth-like planet would have been in serious trouble.

Earth, it appears, is fortunate in being placed right in the middle of a "habitable zone" around our star.

These considerations greatly reduce the number of potentially life-friendly planets per solar system. And there is more. In his 1971 book *Chance and Necessity*, Jacques Monod drew our attention to how unlikely it is that all the ingredients for life just happened to come together in the right order to make the acids and proteins necessary. Serum albumin, for instance, has amino acids in a certain order that would occur in only a vanishingly small number of random cases—what Monod called "chance caught on the wing."

And even if the preconditions for life should occur as a one in many billions chance, the difference between primitive microbes—prokaryotes—and even just more advanced microbes—eukaryotes—is surprisingly complex. Today's prokaryotes (bacteria) haven't changed much in 3 billion years. Only eukaryotes (to which humans are linked) have evolved into complexity. It is quite possible that habitable planets teeming with life exist in other parts of the universe, but that that life is little more than mold.

We are today left with the unpalatable but rational conclusion that instead of Carl Sagan's millions of civilizations, there is a very good chance we are the only one.

Intelligence and technology may be similarly rare. Speech, for instance, which appears to be pretty important in both factors, exists in only one of the 50 billion species on Earth. It is quite possible, then, that we are the only civilization around at the moment.

All this, of course, assumes that life elsewhere is as we know it. It may be that life can arise according to a fundamentally different biology. While possible, such speculation leaves science behind. For life as we know it, we are today left with the unpalatable but rational conclusion that instead of Carl Sagan's millions of civilizations, there is a very good chance we are the only one. The latest decade's discoveries and arguments do not mean that we are alone for certain, but they are probabilities that point strongly in that direction.

Those who want to believe sometimes argue that the mathematical probabilities against intelligent life may be less certain than we think. They cite "complexity theory"—which suggests there may be a certain irregularity and unpredictability even in the laws of nature. But others think the mathematical odds must be respected. "Nobody knows why equations work so well in describing things. Maybe it's the handprint of God, or an ancient, advanced, powerful alien race," says NASA [National Aeronautics and Space Administration] scientist David Grinspoon, but "there is something spooky about the way mathematical relationships are so enmeshed with the physical nature of our universe." For the moment, cold rationality suggests that Jacques Monod was right when he said that "Man at last knows he is alone in the unfeeling immensity of the universe, out of which he has emerged only by chances."

Organizations to Contact

The editors have compiled the following list of organizations concerned with the issues debated in this book. The descriptions are derived from materials provided by the organizations. All have publications or information available for interested readers. The list was compiled on the date of publication of the present volume; the information provided here may change. Be aware that many organizations take several weeks or longer to respond to inquiries, so allow as much time as possible.

Citizens for Space Exploration
PO Box 58724, Houston, TX   77258-8724
(832) 536-3255
website: www.citizensforspaceexploration.org

Citizens for Space Exploration is a coalition of private citizens, small businesses, students, teachers, public officials, and other individuals who are interested in promoting the continuation of space exploration as policy by the US government. Members of the organization travel annually to Washington, D.C., to emphasize the benefits and necessity of funding national space exploration programs. Information about this annual trip can be found on the organization's website.

European Space Agency (ESA)
8, 10 rue Mario-Nikis, Paris   F-75738 Cedex 15
   France
+33 (0) 1 5369 7155 • fax: +33 (0) 1 5369 7690
website: www.esa.int

Headquartered in Paris, France, the European Space Agency is a collective of eighteen member nations funding various space projects. The organization promotes space exploration and shares costs of manned and unmanned missions into space.

The ESA website features educational articles and photo galleries concerning space science and technology as well as analyses of the benefits the organization brings to Europe.

Explore Mars
e-mail: info@ExploreMars.org
website: www.exploremars.org

Explore Mars is a nonprofit organization dedicated to fostering private sector research and development by both scientists and "citizen scientists" related to the exploration of Mars. The organization provides technology innovation awards, sponsors scientific symposiums and workshops, and provides technology demonstrations, all with the hope that creative individuals will develop technologies that will be useful in future journeys to the red planet. Information about current initiatives and a media archive can be found on the Explore Mars website.

Federal Aviation Administration (FAA)
800 Independence Ave. SW, Washington, DC   20591
(866) 835-5322
website: www.faa.gov

The Federal Aviation Administration is the government agency charged with regulating air travel in the United States. As commercial space travel becomes a reality, the FAA also is the agency charged with ensuring the safe operation of this burgeoning industry. The FAA has already published *Concept Operations for Commercial Space Transportation (CST) in the National Airspace System (NAS) Version 2* and *Point-to-Point Commercial Space Transportation in National Aviation System: Final Report* to lay out a regulatory framework for commercial space travel.

Lunar and Planetary Institute (LPI)
3600 Bay Area Blvd., Houston, TX   77058
(281) 486-2100
e-mail: webmaster@lpi.usra.edu
website: www.lpi.usra.edu

The Lunar and Planetary Institute was founded in 1968 to be a central research agency that facilitates cooperation among scientists to enhance understanding of the universe. The three main areas on which the institute focuses are research science, service to the National Aeronautics and Space Administration (NASA) and the planetary science community, and education and public outreach. Through these efforts, LPI seeks to foster communication among scientists and the public and encourage excitement about space research and exploration. The organization's website provides numerous resources, including e-books such as *The Soviet Reach for the Moon* and *Moon Trip: A Personal Account of the Apollo Program and Its Science*, planetary journals, and planetary maps and images.

Mars Society

PO Box 176, McVille, ND 58254
e-mail: info@marssociety.org
website: www.marssociety.org

The Mars Society is a nonprofit organization dedicated to promoting the exploration and permanent settlement of Mars. As such, the society engages in public outreach to encourage and aid Mars pioneers, seeks global support for the government funding of research, and encourages private sector involvement in exploration and settlement. Additionally, the society funds the Mars Desert Research Station and the Flashline Mars Arctic Research Station, which were established to prepare individuals to explore Mars. The Mars Society website provides detailed information about these and other projects.

National Aeronautics and Space Administration (NASA)

Public Communications Office, NASA Headquarters
Suite 5K39, Washington, DC 20546-0001
(202) 358-0001 • fax: (202) 358-4338
website: www.nasa.gov

The National Aeronautics and Space Administration was established in 1958 by President Dwight D. Eisenhower to be a central government organization in charge of flight technology. President John F. Kennedy more specifically focused the organization on sending humans to the moon. After landing men on the moon in 1969, NASA focused on developing a reusable space shuttle that could make multiple trips into space; since its development, the space shuttle has made 120 successful flights into space. Current NASA research has focused on exploring Mars and continuing research here on Earth. Information about current NASA projects and the organization's history can be found on the NASA website.

National Space Society (NSS)

1155 15th St. NW, Suite 500, Washington, DC   20005
(202) 429-1600 • fax: (202) 530-0659
e-mail: nsshq@nss.org
website: www.nss.org

A grassroots, nonprofit organization, the National Space Society works to promote space travel and the expansion of human civilization beyond the Earth. The society maintains that space exploration and colonization are necessary to ensure the survival of the human race in the face of increasing threats on Earth. Additional information justifying the importance of space travel, space settlements, space tourism, the moon, and other topics can be found on the NSS website and in the organization's quarterly journal *Ad Astra*.

SETI Institute

189 Bernardo Ave., Suite 100, Mountain View, CA   94043
(650) 961-6633 • fax: (650) 961-7099
e-mail: info@seti.org
website: www.seti.org

The SETI Institute is a private nonprofit organization founded with the goal of researching, discovering, and explicating the origin, nature and prevalence of life in the universe. SETI stands for Search for Extraterrestrial Intelligence. Since its founding in 1984, SETI scientists have been working to achieve their goals in coordination with NASA and other private space exploration and science organizations. One of the major branches of the organization is the Carl Sagan Center for the Study of Life in the Universe, which is an umbrella for other projects such as "The Formation and Evolution of Planetary Systems: Placing Our Solar System in Context," "Martian Surface Composition and Its Practical Applications to Astrobiology," and "From Habitability to Life." Information about these projects and others as well as education and outreach materials can be accessed on the organization's website.

Space Frontier Foundation
16 First Ave., Nyack, NY   10960
e-mail: info@spacefrontier.org
website: www.spacefrontier.org

The Space Frontier Foundation has been working since 1988 to advocate for the expansion of humanity into permanent settlements in space. The foundation's mission is based on the belief that space offers the unlimited resources necessary for the continued survival of the human race for countless generations. With its conferences, speakers, policy papers, and projects, this organization continues to work to inform both policymakers and the public about the importance of space exploration and colonization. Articles detailing this mission and efforts to accomplish it can be found on the organization's website, under the title SpaceFront.

Bibliography

Books

Paula Berinstein   *Making Space Happen: Private Space Ventures and the Visionaries Behind Them*. Melford, NJ: Plexus, 2002.

Joan Lisa Bromberg   *NASA and the Space Industry*. Baltimore, MD: Johns Hopkins University Press, 1999.

Michael Carroll   *The Seventh Landing: Going Back to the Moon, This Time to Stay*. New York: Springer, 2009.

Paul Davies   *The Eerie Silence: Renewing Our Search for Alien Intelligence*. Boston, MA: Houghton Mifflin, 2010.

Paul Gilster   *Centauri Dreams: Imagining and Planning Interstellar Exploration*. New York: Copernicus, 2004.

J. Richard Gott and Robert J. Vanderbei   *Sizing Up the Universe: The Cosmos in Perspective*. Washington, DC: National Geographic, 2010.

Brian Harvey   *Europe's Space Programme: To Ariane and Beyond*. New York: Springer, 2003.

Brian Harvey, Henk H.F. Smid, and Theo Pirard   *Emerging Space Powers: The New Space Programs of Asia, the Middle East and South America*. New York: Springer, 2010.

Edward L. Hudgins	*Space: The Free-Market Frontier.* Washington, DC: Cato Institute, 2002.
Joan Johnson-Freese	*Space as a Strategic Asset.* New York: Columbia University Press, 2007.
W.D. Kay	*Defining NASA: The Historical Debate over the Agency's Mission.* Albany, NY: State University of New York Press, 2005.
Kenny Kemp	*Destination Space: Making Science Fiction a Reality.* London, England: Virgin, 2010.
Howard E. McCurdy	*Faster, Better, Cheaper: Low-Cost Innovation in the U.S. Space Program.* Baltimore, MD: Johns Hopkins University Press, 2001.
Joseph N. Pelton and Angelia P. Bukley, eds.	*The Farthest Shore: A 21st Century Guide to Space.* Burlington, Canada: Collector's Guide, 2010.
Mary Roach	*Packing for Mars: The Curious Science of Life in the Void.* New York: Norton, 2010.
Carl Sagan	*Pale Blue Dot: A Vision of the Human Future in Space.* New York: Ballantine, 1997.
Stanley Schmidt	*Islands in the Sky: Bold New Ideas for Colonizing Space.* Hoboken, NJ: John Wiley & Sons, 1996.

Stephen Webb   *If the Universe Is Teeming with Aliens . . . Where Is Everybody? Fifty Solutions to Fermi's Paradox and the Problem of Extraterrestrial Life.* New York: Copernicus, 2002.

Robert Zimmerman   *Leaving Earth: Space Stations, Rival Superpowers, and the Quest for Interplanetary Travel.* Washington, DC: Joseph Henry, 2006.

Robert Zubrin   *Entering Space: Creating a Spacefaring Civilization.* New York: Jeremy P. Tarcher/Putnam, 1999.

Periodicals

Bill Andrews   "What Are Galaxies Trying to Tell Us?," *Astronomy*, February 2011.

Stephen Baird   "Space: The New Frontier!," *Technology Teacher*, April 2008.

Peter Dickens   "The Humanization of the Cosmos—To What End?," *Monthly Review: An Independent Socialist Magazine*, November 2010.

Richard Docksai   "Down-to-Earth NASA," *Futurist*, July/August 2010.

Alan W. Dowd   "Surrendering Outer Space," *Policy Review*, August/September 2009.

David H. Freedman   "Jump-Starting the Orbital Economy," *Scientific American*, December 2010.

John Hart — "Cosmic Commons: Contact and Community," *Theology & Science*, November 2010.

Michael D. Lemonick — "Is Anybody out There?," *Time*, November 8, 2010.

Kate Lunau — "Destination Mars," *Maclean's*, September 27, 2010.

Kelly Melone — "Redefining Exploration: The Future Utilization of the International Space Station," *Ad Astra*, Winter 2010.

Guy Norris — "Galactic Quest," *Aviation Week & Space Technology*, September 7, 2009.

Jonathan Penn — "NASA's Plan Is Not Sustainable," *Aviation Week & Space Technology*, December 6, 2010.

Elizabeth Quill — "Can You Hear Me Now?" *Science News*, April 24, 2010.

Andrew Romano and Fred Guterl — "Aliens Exist," *Newsweek*, August 24, 2009.

Harrison H. Schmitt — "From the Moon," *Scientific American*, July 2009.

David Shiga — "Space 2020: What NASA Will Do Next," *New Scientist*, February 13, 2010.

Sanjoy Som — "An International Symbol for the Sustained Exploration of Space," *Space Policy*, August 2010.

Lynda Williams   "Irrational Dreams of Space Colonization," *Peace Review*, January–March 2010.

Mark Williamson   "Planetary Protection: Contaminate or Conserve?" *Ad Astra*, Winter 2010.

Robert Zubrin   "Wrecking NASA," *Commentary*, June 2010.

Index